INTERIOR INSPIRATION
SCANDINAVIA

SONIA LUCANO

INTERIOR INSPIRATION
SCANDINAVIA

Thames & Hudson

With over 150 illustrations

CON.

06

.TENTS

- 105

PART TWO: PRACTICAL PROJECTS

INTRODUCTION

Practicality + sustainability + aestheticism

Scandinavian design is rooted in a particular set of ideals: the desire to create beautiful, everyday objects that are practical, affordable and suitable for mass production. This desire underpins the concept of 'democratic design' that first emerged in Scandinavia during the 1930s, and which related to the production of functionally and aesthetically pleasing objects for the home, such as furniture, textiles and kitchenware.

Consequently, the five Scandinavian countries - Denmark, Finland, Norway, Sweden and Iceland - all share a distinct visual culture. Their designs are dictated by common sense, a practical spirit and a wish to make beautiful objects that are accessible to all.

IKEA, the very emblem of Swedish design, perhaps expresses this philosophy best, claiming 'democratic design' as the ideal 'combination of form, function, quality, sustainability and a low price'.

← **Arne Jacobsen** • The Swan • Made by Fritz Hansen • 1958

OVERVIEW

Ø1. THE HISTORY OF SCANDINAVIAN DESIGN

THE SCANDINAVIAN PHILOSOPHY

Functionalism, the simplification of form...the democratization of design, all devoted to improving the quality of everyday life.

Modern Scandinavian design was born in the 1930s, an era in which young artists and designers were beginning to set out as their goals functionalism, the simplification of form and, in particular, the democratization of design, all devoted to improving the quality of everyday life.

The term 'Scandinavian design' - first coined during the 1950s, following an exhibition that toured the U.S. and Canada - has now become synonymous with this democratic attitude. It implies simple and accessible products inspired by nature, as well as an emphasis on taking pleasure in the domestic environment.

This philosophy can be easily understood if we consider the geography and climate of this part of the world. The weather in Scandinavia is often extreme: it can be exceptionally cold, the days are short in winter and there is little light. Scandinavians, therefore, tend to centre their focus on their homes, which can provide them with comfort and a sense of wellbeing.

A Danish word that is difficult to define perfectly expresses this outlook: *hygge* (pronounced 'hoo-ga'). One might translate it as meaning 'cosiness', or as a feeling of wellbeing, homeliness or relaxation, the desire to create a comforting atmosphere that results in an experience that is simple yet has a profound impact on wellbeing. *Hygge* - candlelight, being with family and friends, enjoying good food and conversation, in sum, the small pleasures - could be the best weapon against the long, dark Scandinavian winters. This modest word might explain why Danish people are considered to be the happiest in the world.

Such is the context and the spirit in which Scandinavian designers have always worked. Theirs is a quest to find means of lightening the everyday gloom.

Design is integral to the daily life of Scandinavians. Its play a central role in the balance between the pleasures of nature, with its wide open spaces, and those of the home, a warm and cosy cocoon in which people can escape from the harsher elements of the natural world that surrounds them.

WHAT IS SCANDINAVIAN DESIGN?

14

Scandinavian design, then, is a marvellous mixture of the functional and the aesthetic, and defined by ideals that are common to all the Nordic countries: a practical outlook, social conscience, respect for the environment and aesthetic sensitivity.

As such, it aims to improve quality of life through the use of natural products and materials, continuous research into new design technologies and the underlying awareness that all objects must be affordable, factors that are apparent across all areas of design, whether furniture, textiles, lighting or kitchenware.

A practical outlook, social conscience, respect for the environment and aesthetic sensitivity.

Being environmentally conscious, Scandinavian design involves the use of natural renewable resources that are available locally, and so wood is a material very common (it also provides the feeling of warmth that is so essential to *hygge*). Other resources that are prevalent include rattan and leather. The Nordic countries are not overly blessed with natural resources, and so it is a basic principle that their reserves - above all, their forests - must be carefully managed. Sustainability is another offshoot of this ethic.

There is also deep respect for traditional techniques. A typical example is the art of blown glass, examples of which are to be found everywhere.

→ **Finn Juhl** • 108 Dining Chairs • Made by Onecollection • 1946

Designers also frequently draw their inspiration from nature: forms are curved, the motifs found in textiles derived from flora and fauna, though these are often presented in a simplified, or abstract, way. A prime consideration for every designer is that whatever they create, it must be done with a meticulous and sensitive spirit. A Swedish slogan follows the same path: *'Vackrare vardagsvara'* ('Something beautiful for every day').

Cost is another all-important factor: the work must be as widely accessible as possible. But although cost, practicality, sustainability and aesthetics are all part of the package, so too is art for art's sake. There are all manner of objects that are made purely for visual appeal rather than for function. Even these will eventually find their way into mass production.

'Something beautiful for every day'

THE GOLDEN AGE OF SCANDINAVIAN DESIGN

Scandinavian design hit its peak between the 1930s and the 1960s, which is when its popularity was first felt across the globe. Since then, Scandinavian talents have continued to make their mark internationally, and are still at the forefront of aesthetic developments. That is why, even now, Scandinavian design is a byword for iconic design.

The first generation of designers that enjoyed worldwide recognition included Arne Jacobsen, Verner Panton and Alvar Aalto. It was they who established the fundamental values that are still at the heart of contemporary Scandinavian design.

Such is the longevity of their work that many of their pieces are still in production today. And their influence can still be felt in the output of contemporary designers from all over the world.

← **Arne Jacobsen** • The Swan • Made by Fritz Hansen • 1958

02. THE FIVE SCANDINAVIAN COUNTRIES AND THEIR UNIQUE FEATURES

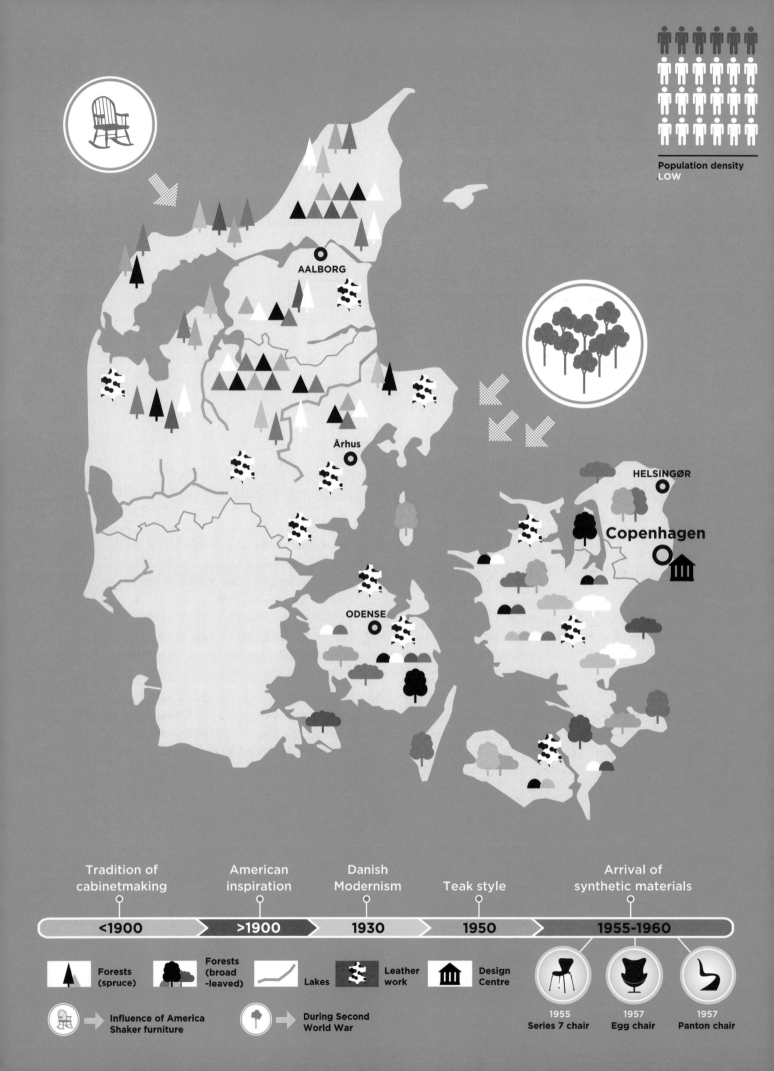

AALBORG

Århus

HELSINGØR

Copenhagen

ODENSE

Population density
LOW

Tradition of
cabinetmaking

American
inspiration

Danish
Modernism

Teak style

Arrival of
synthetic materials

<1900   >1900   1930   1950   1955-1960

Forests
(spruce)

Forests
(broad
-leaved)

Lakes

Leather
work

Design
Centre

Influence of America
Shaker furniture

During Second
World War

1955
Series 7 chair

1957
Egg chair

1957
Panton chair

DENMARK

Although only a small country with a tiny population, Denmark has played a major role in the history of arts and crafts since the mid-twentieth century. The artistic tradition of the country stems from a particular constraint to which the Danes have had to adapt quickly: the lack of a wide range of raw materials. As such they have had to make full use of the resources that are readily available, such as wood and leather, to perfect their means of exploiting them in their art and craft. Practicality and sustainability are prime requirements, leading to a style simple and understated, with the emphasis being on functionality.

Danish people have a long tradition of cabinetmaking and, since the 1930s, have produced very simple but elegant furniture in this form. From early on, out of necessity as well as taste, their favoured material has been wood. A respect for nature can clearly be seen in their works, which show a predilection for organic shapes, as can a pursuit of ideal forms, defined by gentle lines and curves.

The Danes are always ready and willing to look beyond their own shores for inspiration, and during the twentieth century they were influenced by the ultra simple, old-fashioned aestheticism of the American Shakers. Designers such as Børge Mogensen and Hans Wegner, in particular, drew on this style in their work.

Danish Modernism rapidly became synonymous with good taste, and was the precursor of 'good design' all across Scandinavia. The products were exhibited and exported to Europe and the U.S. throughout the 1950s, and 'Made in Denmark' became an aesthetic hallmark all over the world.

At that time, Danish designers very often used teak - a durable, high-quality material - in their furniture, a choice that might seem strange given that it is a wood not native to the country. However, huge quantities of the wood had in fact been felled to clear way for military operations in the Philippines during the Second World War, after which it was imported into the country. Peter Hvidt, Hans Wegner and Finn Juhl made great use of teak in their furniture, and it also formed the basis of decorative pieces and objects for everyday use, such as Jen Quistgaard's celebrated ice bucket. Once again, these designers followed the principles of low cost and a respect for natural resources in their use of this fine but inexpensive wood.

The year 1955 marked a turning point in Danish design, signalled by the first experiments in the use of moulded plywood. This was typical of the Scandinavian predilection for trying out new materials and technologies. It was Arne Jacobsen who paved the way with his famous Series 7 chair (model No. 3107), which became a veritable icon of Danish design. It is still one of the best-selling models in the world, and a staple for many major retailers of home ware.

The combination of natural and synthetic materials opened up new avenues: fibreglass and latex brought new impetus, and designers now began to distance themselves from the slightly outmoded *Shaker* spirit. Arne Jacobsen continued on in his pioneering way, producing his iconic Egg chair in 1957, and Verner Panton achieved a spectacular breakthrough with his Panton chair, the first to be moulded in plastic, and in psychedelic shapes and colours. Soon after, in 1978, the Danish Design Centre was founded in Copenhagen, whose aim it was to develop the distribution and economic exploitation of Danish creativity.

Today, like the rest of the world, Denmark is profoundly affected by the diminution of natural resources and other environmental problems. And so now more than ever it stays faithful to its ethical values and to the humanist principles that have always characterized its design.

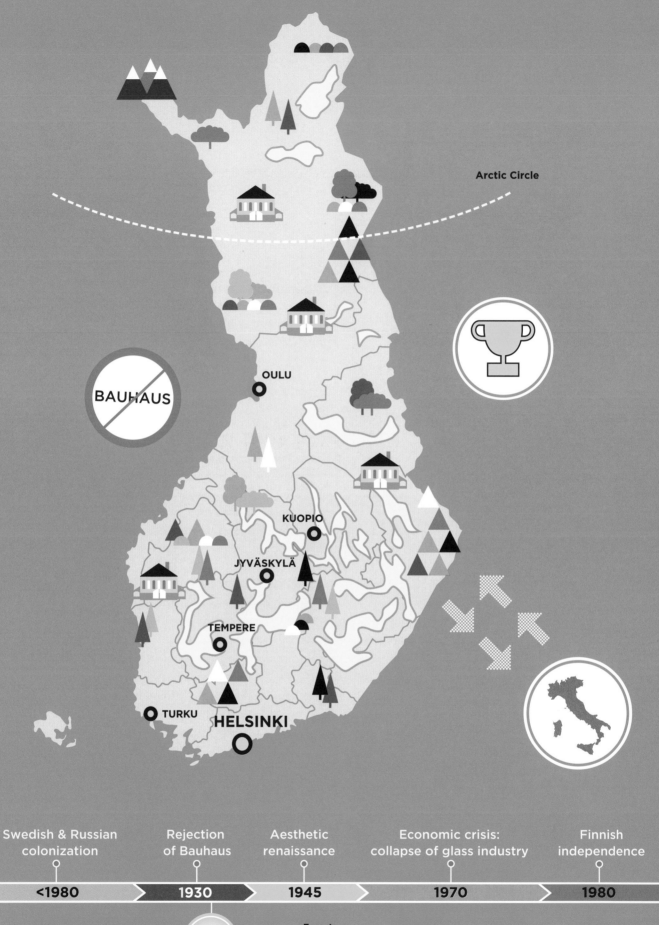

Arctic Circle

BAUHAUS

OULU

KUOPIO

JYVÄSKYLÄ

TEMPERE

TURKU

HELSINKI

1950: awards for glassware
at Milan Triennal

Close ties between Italian
& Finnish designers

1936
Savoy Vase

Forests
(broad
-leaved)

Forests
(spruce)

Lakes

Manufacture
of glassware

Mountains

FINLAND

The Finns, like many of their Scandinavian neighbours, have always had to fight for survival against the extreme elements of nature. This is especially true of the northern regions of the country, which are situated in the Arctic Circle. Like their neighbours, the Finns have a profound love and respect for the wildness and beauty of their homeland, and its severe climate.

To survive, they have been forced to develop their own innate sense of efficiency, and to adapt to the demands of their natural environment: the Finns are renowned for their strength of character and their endurance. And so it is hardly surprising that their designs are made in close harmony with nature, both in form and material.

Finnish design tends to comprise unique, ornamental pieces, and in this regard it differs from the other Nordic countries in its focus and in its notion of democracy. However, it often happens that these experimental objects eventually make their way into mass production, even if that was not the original intention.

Finnish designers are passionate for *objets d'art* as luxury goods. Ceramic and glass manufacturers such as Arabia and Iittala typify this trend, while still preserving the traditional techniques of craftsmanship.

Together with nature, the country's political history has been a powerful influence on the temperament of the Finnish people. They have almost always fallen under the dominion of other countries: first Sweden, and then Russia. Not until 1980 did Finland finally regain full autonomy, following a long struggle for independence. It is from this desire for autonomy that a particular cultural identity has emerged, as well as a focus on making a distinctive mark in their art, one that distinguishes them not only from their Nordic neighbours but from the rest of the world.

Alvar Aalto is one of the key proponents of Finnish design. In 1930, he followed the example of his contemporaries and turned his back on the cold sterility of the Bauhaus movement, devoting himself instead to the organic forms to be found in the Finnish landscape. It was at this time that he created the famous Savoy Vase (also known as the Aalto Vase), directly inspired by the curved shores of the lakes all around.

The unique nature of Finnish design has also come about through exchanges with designers further afield than Scandinavia. In 1930, Arttu Brummer - the managing director and editor-in-chief of the Italian magazine *Domus* - developed close ties between Italian and Finnish designers, whereby the latter were greatly enriched by the ideas of the former.

After the Second World War, Finland experienced a great renaissance through designers such as Tapio Wirkkala and Timo Sarpaneva, heralding the dawn of a new aestheticism. At the Milan Triennale in 1950 awards were won by Finnish designers. They were noted in particular for their exceptional glassware, and this gave a major boost to their confidence. Described as 'a mixture of primitive audacity and incredible elegance', through such work the Finns had at last achieved the autonomy to which they had aspired for so long, and this was now being recognized internationally.

During the 1970s the worldwide economic crisis had damaging repercussions on the glass industry. Subsequently, the Finns turned to designs that were more amenable to new technologies, although they always retained their close ties with nature.

Today, the more established manufacturers, such as Iittala and Arabia, still lead the way, attracting the big names in contemporary design. Finnish design remains faithful, however, to its spiritual origins, with its emphasis being still on national identity and the balance between form, function and materials.

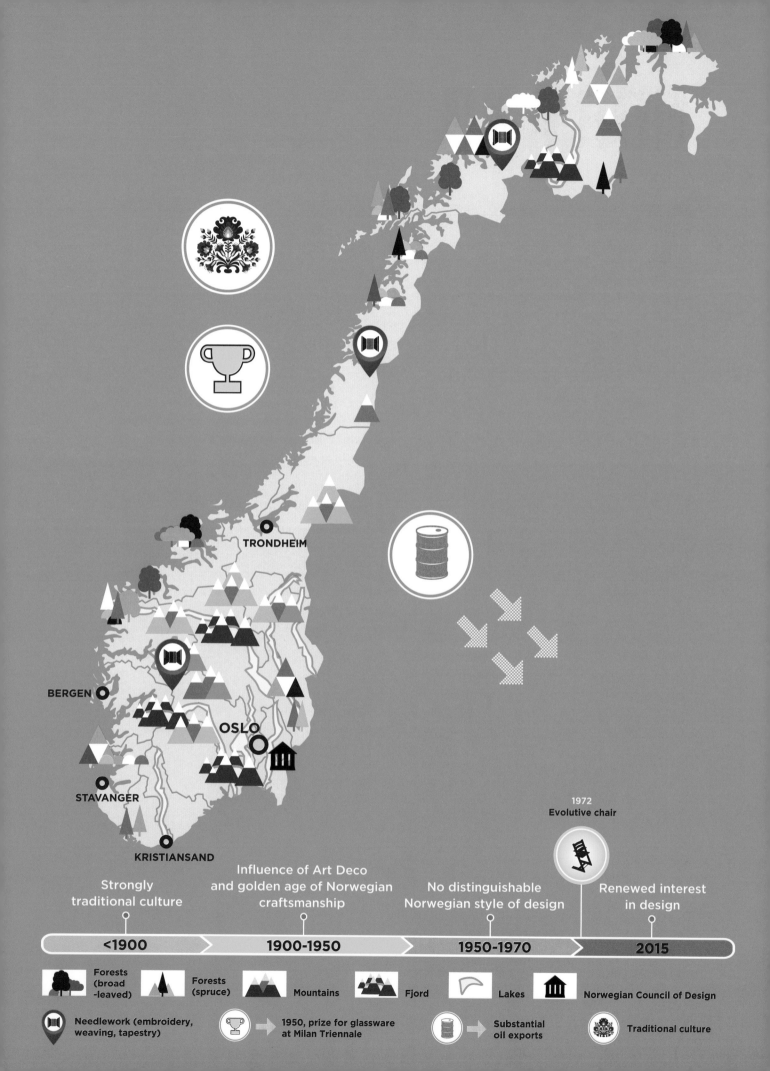

TRONDHEIM

BERGEN

OSLO

STAVANGER

KRISTIANSAND

1972
Evolutive chair

Strongly
traditional culture

Influence of Art Deco
and golden age of Norwegian
craftsmanship

No distinguishable
Norwegian style of design

Renewed interest
in design

<1900   1900-1950   1950-1970   2015

Forests
(broad
-leaved)   Forests
(spruce)   Mountains   Fjord   Lakes   Norwegian Council of Design

Needlework (embroidery,
weaving, tapestry)   1950, prize for glassware
at Milan Triennale   Substantial
oil exports   Traditional culture

NORWAY

Norwegian landscape is a sublime mixture of mountains, forests and fjords. Its people are scattered over an immense area, which in former times made contact with others and the outside world difficult; this may explain why Norwegians developed a form of autocracy as early as 1814. Their agricultural infrastructure, which flourishes in finer weather, allows them a degree of autonomy from their neighbours, while the long, hard winters they spend embellishing their homes, with a particular focus on textile work: weaving, embroidery and tapestry-making.

Folklore and tradition have always played an important role in Norwegian visual culture, with a profound respect for both being expressed by designers. Colours too are important, and typically drawn from nature: red, brown and russet are omnipresent, even in architecture - as can be seen, for example, in the weatherboard facades so characteristic of the country.

Nature is also the inspiration for the motifs found in Norwegian design, and is particularly prevalent in enamel work, glassware, textiles and tapestries. These were executed with great delicacy by such artists as Gustav Gaudernack, whose enamel bowls were decorated with dragonflies and plant arabesques, or by Frida Hansen, who made textiles and tapestries incorporating floral designs.

The 1920s saw the foundation of the Landsforbundet Norsk Brukskunst. This institution brought together craftsmen and designers with the aim of establishing a national identity in the context of design, and comprised makers of unique studio pieces along with designers of work that could be mass-produced.

From 1950 Norwegian designers began to gain international recognition, one of them being Willy Johansson, who was awarded a prize for his glassware at the Milan Triennale. There were other individual successes, but in general Norwegian designers never achieved the heights attained by their neighbours. Even while the period from 1930 to 1960 was the golden age of Scandinavian design, the Norwegians were still in the process of establishing their identity. A few exceptions did emerge, including Peter Opsvik and his Evolutive Chair in 1972, but even to this day there is no truly recognizable Norwegian style. Instead the county has become better known for its industry in oil exports and its exploitation of the resources of the North Sea.

However, with oil revenues now dwindling, there is a renewed interest in design. This can be seen in the establishment of the Norsk Designerad, or Norwegian Council of Design, whose mission is to promote design products by local makers and to find outlets for them abroad. Norwegian designers continue to combine art and technology, and to create innovative work that can compete with that of their Nordic neighbours.

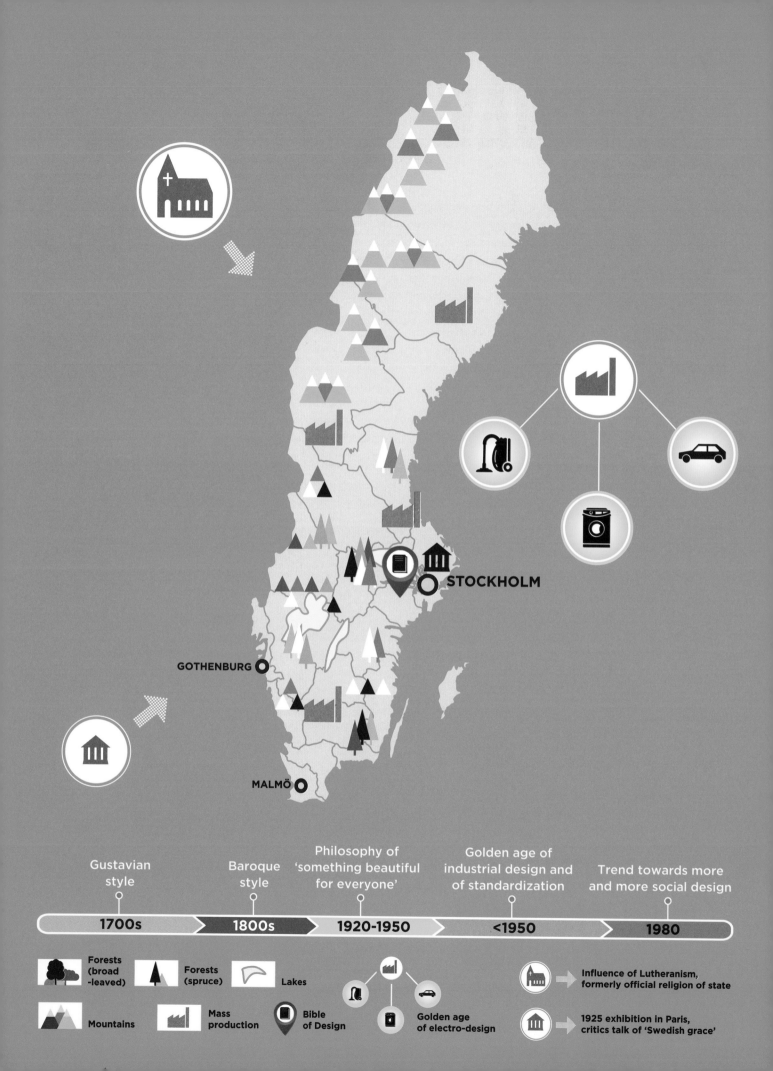

STOCKHOLM

GOTHENBURG

MALMÖ

Gustavian
style

Baroque
style

Philosophy of
'something beautiful
for everyone'

Golden age of
industrial design and
of standardization

Trend towards more
and more social design

1700s   **1800s**   **1920-1950**   **<1950**   **1980**

Forests
(broad
-leaved)

Forests
(spruce)

Lakes

Mountains

Mass
production

Bible
of Design

Golden age
of electro-design

Influence of Lutheranism,
formerly official religion of state

1925 exhibition in Paris,
critics talk of 'Swedish grace'

SWEDEN

Sweden is the largest of the five Scandinavian countries. The land alternates dramatically between forests, mountains and plains, like a multitude of small islands. The Swedes themselves have a very strong community spirit, which can undoubtedly be traced back to the prevailing religion of the country, Lutheranism. The ideology of these people is a subtle blend of collective responsibility and individual freedom, and this plays a major part in their brand of creativity, reinforcing the social aspect of their design.

During the late eighteenth century, the Swedes developed a particular aesthetic of their own, which was known as the 'Gustavian style'. It was exported all over the world - especially to France - and harked back to classicism with its characteristic simplicity and use of pastel shades. Everything was light and gentle, and the purity could be partly attributed to a lack of materials: unable to import the nobler woods, the Swedes began to use painted pine for their furniture. Another factor was certainly the ethic of modesty and sobriety that is still so prevalent in Swedish society. The mid-nineteenth century, however, saw the appearance of all kinds of ornamentation, with the result being a style that was more heavily laden with motifs and pattern to the point of becoming almost baroque.

At the beginning of the twentieth century, the Swedish writer Ellen Key was advancing the idea that one must resolve social problems by creating beautiful objects: 'A beautiful domestic environment can only contribute to making people happier.'

In 1917 an 'Ideal Homes Exhibition' was held in Stockholm, giving full expression to Key's ideas. Among the exhibits was the *Arbetarservisen*, designed by Wilhelm Käge, a dinner service for workers, decorated with blue lilies. The new Swedish creed was born: 'Something beautiful for everyone'.

This crockery was the first mass-produced product to reflect most effectively the Scandinavian ideal of functionality married to aestheticism. The exhibition was a turning point in Swedish design, and it reinforced the general aim to create high-quality objects at low prices.

In 1925, the '*Exposition internationale des arts décoratifs et industriels modernes*' in Paris gave prominence to Swedish designs, which were noted for their simple, elegant style. One critic spoke of 'Swedish grace', and so it made its mark on the international scene.

In 1950, there was a return to simplicity, which once more became the basic feature of Swedish design, in the tradition of the Gustavian style. But now more than ever, it aspired to social equality, following a concept that led to ever greater standardization of products. That was one of the consequences of prioritizing functionality and low cost in order to make them accessible to all. Ikea is perhaps the best example: this company is the very embodiment of the drive to export contemporary Swedish design at its cheapest and most functional.

Architecture and design reflected Swedish democracy and its ethos, and houses, objects, furniture, and so on, all followed the norm.

However, some designers resisted the trend: Josef Frank, for instance, insisted that 'there is no unique principle in matters of good interior design'. More and more designers joined him in lamenting the absence of the Swedish character in design.

29

↓ **Arne Jacobsen** • The Drop • Made by Fritz Hansen • 1958

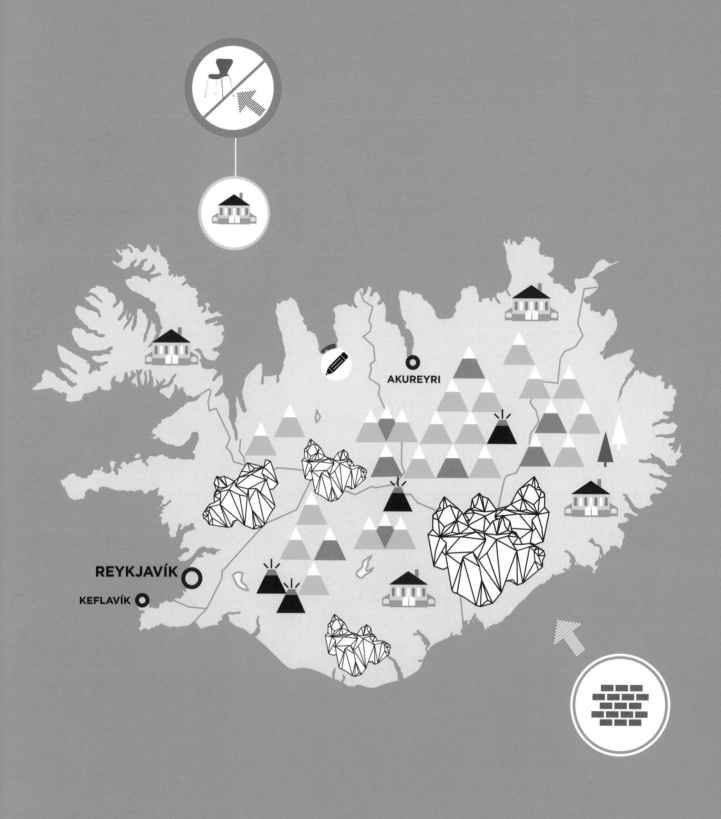

AKUREYRI

REYKJAVÍK

KEFLAVÍK

Emergence of
Icelandic identity

Independence

New creations resulting from
ban on importation of furniture

Design geared to use
of new technologies

Between the wars | **1944** | **1950-1960** | **2015**

 Glaciers   Mountains   Volcanoes   Forests (spruce)   Lakes   Furniture factories

 1930: import of cement and concrete

 1950-1960: ban on import of furniture leads to opening of furniture factories

 Outstanding in field of graphic design

ICELAND

Iceland is a unique country - an island whose landscapes alternate between vast glaciers, volcanoes and mountain peaks. The land has always presented massive problems of adaptation in the great struggle for survival, and so it is little wonder that its people have a reputation for being so hardy. They have also had to fight time and again in order to keep and regain their independence.

In spite of the geographical and political hardships, Icelanders have succeeded in forging their own identity between the two world wars, both in architecture and design.

Iceland is almost devoid of any natural building material. There are very few forests, and the importation of pinewood would have been far too expensive, so the Icelanders have had to turn elsewhere for resources with which to construct their homes. Cement, which is easy to transport and to use, has been a principal component. During the 1930s, their main material was moulded concrete, which they put to use especially in their architecture.

The Icelanders obtained their independence in 1944, and this saw the birth of a new identity. They became particularly prominent in the field of graphic design.

During the 1950s, there was a ban on the import of furniture, and this led to the opening up of numerous small factories whose task it was to provide furniture for local homes. The result was many fine creations, such as Gunnar Magnússon's set of table and chairs.

Icelanders specialize in readapting existing forms, which itself can lead to a highly original treatment of these objects.

Today, Icelandic design is increasingly geared to new technologies, such as laser-cutting in the textile industry. But at the same time, this country's designers zealously preserve the traditional skills of their ancestors.

Ø3.
THE ICONS OF SCANDINAVIAN DESIGN

Aino Aalto	**Eero Aarnio**	
54	5Ø	
		Carl-Axel Acking
Alvar Aalto		42
38		
Lis Ahlmann	**Erik Gunnar Asplund**	
52	38	
		Sigvard Bernadotte
Folke Arström		58
58		
	Nanna & Jørgen Ditzel	
Bing & Grøndahl		
54	46	
		Kaj Franck
Acton Bjørn		59
56		
Søren Hansen	**Göran Hongell**	
4Ø	56	
		Saara Hopea
Poul Henningsen		62
56		
Peter Hvidt	**Arne Jacobsen**	
42	38	
		Jacob Jensen
Maija Isola		62
53		
Finn Juhl	**Poul Kjaerholm**	
45	47	
		Le Klint
Wilhelm Kåge		65
55		
Vibeke Klint	**Yrjö Kukkapuro**	
52	5Ø	
		Stig Lindberg
Henning Koppel		61
61		
Erik Magnussen	**Børge Mogensen**	
64	42	
		Orla Mølgaard-Nielsen
Bruno Mathsson		
4Ø		42
Steen Østergaard	**Jens H. Quistgaard**	
5Ø	62	
		Eero Saarinen
Verner Panton		4Ø
48		
Timo Sarpaneva	**Hans Wegner**	
64	45	
		Tapio Wirkkala
Ilmari Tapiovaara		61
45		

THE DESIGNERS

FURN • ITURE

ERIK GUNNAR ASPLUND (Sweden, 1885–1940)

Although initially a painter, Asplund decided early on to focus entirely on architecture, opening a studio in Stockholm in 1909. He designed many buildings, including the Stockholm Library in 1928, a masterpiece of purity and formal refinement. He also created some outstanding items of furniture, especially chairs in wood or metal, to complement the interiors of his buildings.

ALVAR AALTO (Finland, 1898–1976)

Aalto began his career as a brilliant architect, organic forms in particular being a trademark of his practice. He and his wife, Aino, experimented with the technique of bending wood, which they applied to chairs and then introduced into the international design scene.

Aalto is particularly remembered for his Models No. 31 and 41, which he made during the 1930s and which are still regarded as design icons. He and Aino also experimented with glassware, resulting in another classic - the Savoy Vase in 1936 - which anticipated the organic forms of postwar Scandinavian design.

ARNE JACOBSEN (Denmark, 1902–1971)

Arne Jacobsen graduated in architecture from the Copenhagen Royal Academy of Fine Arts in 1927. For two years he worked as an assistant to Copenhagen's chief architect, and during this period he designed some notable buildings, such as the House of the Future, and he also experimented with furniture design. In 1930, he opened his own agency for design and architecture in Hellerup. He soon obtained several commissions, which included the famous Bellevue Theatre with its seating in bent plywood. He began to design furniture in 1945, not for the interiors of his own buildings but for mass production. He created a series of iconic pieces - such as the Ant chair and the Series 7 Chair, which were generally moulded in plywood and had metal legs - for Fritz Hansen. The designs that he made specifically for his own buildings would also eventually be mass produced: for example, the Egg chair and the Swan chair, which he created for the Royal Hotel in Copenhagen. He also designed lamps for Louis Poulsen and kitchen utensils and cutlery in steel. All of these pieces were highly successful, and his pure, futuristic shapes became the dominant aesthetic of the time.

Arne Jacobsen was the most famous of all Danish architects and designers, and embodied the many outstanding qualities of Scandinavian design.

01. Arne Jacobsen • Grand Prix chair • Made by Fritz Hansen • 1960

02. Arne Jacobsen • Egg chair • Made by Fritz Hansen • 1958

03. Arne Jacobsen • The Swan • 1958 • **Jaime Hayon** • Favn Sofa • 2011 • Both made by Fritz Hansen

04. Erik Gunnar Asplund • Goteborg chair • Made by Cassina Maestri • 1937

05. Alvar Aalto • Paimio armchair No. 14 • 1931

01.

02.

03.

04.

05.

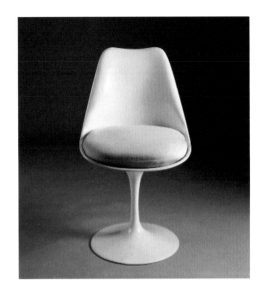

← **Eero Saarinen** • Tulip chair No. 151 •
Made by Kroll International • 1955–1957

SØREN HANSEN (Denmark, 1905–1977)

Søren was the son of the industrialist Fritz Hansen, who founded the company that bears his name. Using the bentwood technique perfected by Thonet in Austria, he created the Dan Chair, a bistro-style chair the back rest and back legs of which are formed from a single piece of wood. Quite apart from its technical mastery, the purity of its curves mark it out as a prime specimen of Scandinavian design. Søren continued the traditions of his father's company by designing numerous chairs, always maintaining a balance between aestheticism and mass production, and continuing to modernize existing models.

BRUNO MATHSSON (Sweden, 1907–1988)

Mathsson learned the art of cabinetmaking from his father. In the early 1930s, he designed furniture mainly for the family firm. He tended to favour organic forms, referring to morphology (the study of the structure of organisms) in particular for inspiration, and he often used straps of leather in the seats of his chairs to accommodate the shape of the sitter. This trend was called 'organic modernism'. He also devoted much of his time to architecture. His designs are still being made and sold by Fritz Hansen.

EERO SAARINEN (Finland, 1910–1961)

At the age of thirteen, Saarinen emigrated with his family to the U.S., where in due course he studied architecture. This remained his principal field of activity, but he also worked as a designer. His most famous creation was the Tulip chair, which has been made by Knoll since 1956.

↑ **Bruno Mathsson** • Super-Circular table • Made by Fritz Hansen • 1968

BØRGE MOGENSEN (Denmark, 1914–1972)

After studying art, Mogensen took up cabinetmaking under the direction of Le Klint. He was profoundly influenced by the American Shaker tradition, and designed the Shaker chair in 1944. Characteristic of his work is his use of high-quality natural materials, including beechwood, and seats made of plant fibre.

PETER HVIDT (Denmark, 1916–1986) AND ORLA MØLGAARD-NIELSEN (Denmark, 1907–1993)

These designers began their long and fruitful collaboration in 1944. Mølgaard-Nielsen started his career as a cabinetmaker, and was well versed in the field of anthropometry (the scientific study of human proportions) whereas Hvidt had studied design in Copenhagen and had worked with several design studios.

The Portex chair was the first product on which they worked: made of teak it was modern and stackable. They produced a variety of work for the great Danish industrialist Fritz Hansen, in particular many items of furniture in laminated wood. In 1947, they created the AX chair, which appeared in a number of materials and models, with and without armrests. With the aim of producing high-quality pieces at low prices they hit on the idea of the AX chair 'kit', in which the constituent pieces were packaged separately and could be assembled at home, thereby reducing the cost of shipping. A best-seller of the 1950s, the AX won several awards and continues to be a design icon.

CARL-AXEL ACKING (Sweden, 1910–2001)

Acking was an architect, who opened his own studio in Stockholm in the early 1940s. He devoted much of his time to interior design, especially within offices, which led to the creation of numerous items of furniture, armchairs and lamps. He was particularly interested in working with bentwood and with combinations of wood and leather.

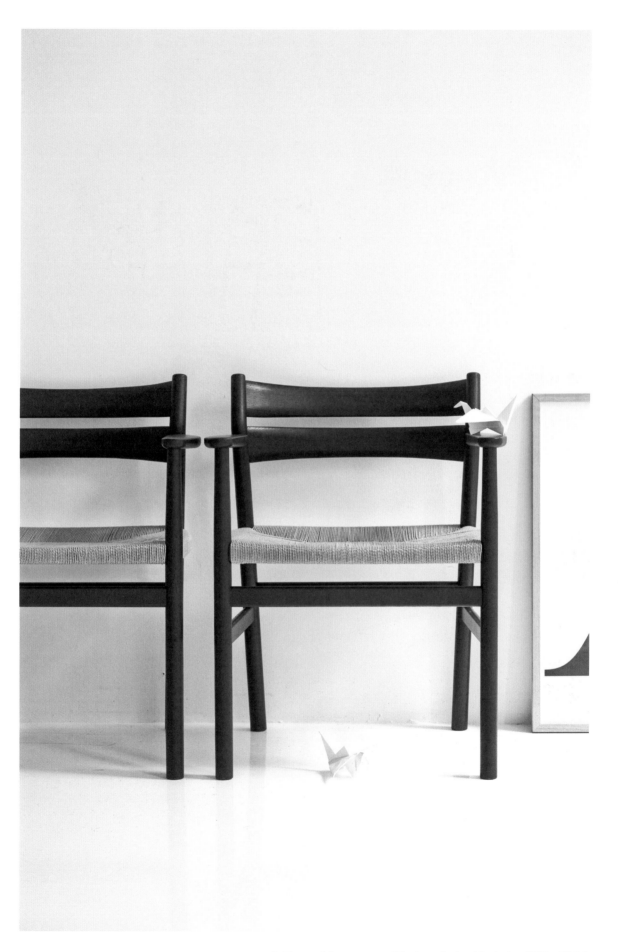

↑ **Børge Mogensen** • Shaker chair • Made by DK3 • 1944

← **Finn Juhl** • Armchair Model No. NV-45 • Made by Niels Vodder • 1945

ILMARI TAPIOVAARA (Finland, 1914–1999)

Tapiovaara began his career at the Aalto's Artek studio, but then returned to Helsinki to study design. After a short spell with Le Corbusier in Paris, he and his wife set up their own design studio, and created the famous stackable Domus chair in moulded plywood. He spent much of his career in pursuit of designing the ideal chair.

FINN JUHL (Denmark, 1912–1989)

After studying architecture in Copenhagen, Juhl began his career in the creative design studio of his professor, Vilhelm Lauritzen. For about ten years, he designed numerous items of furniture, especially chairs, many of which went on to become veritable landmarks in the history of Scandinavian design. His forms are very organic, and his handling of the wooden supports and armrests is almost sculptural.

In 1945, just after the war, he started his own company and again designed a large quantity of chairs, sofas and tables, which won awards at various Milan Triennales and were displayed at many exhibitions. Particularly striking are his NV-45 and NV-48 armchairs for Niels Vodder, again organic forms realized in his favourite material, teak. He led the way in establishing a new style, commonly known as the 'teak style'. As a professor at the Copenhagen School of Interior Design from 1945 to 1955, he would influence a whole generation of designers.

↑ **Hans Wegner** • China chair • Made by Fritz Hansen • 1943

HANS WEGNER (Denmark, 1914–2007)

After serving an apprenticeship in cabinetmaking, Wegner took courses in joinery. During the 1940s, he opened his own studio and designed furniture in collaboration with Børge Mogensen. His furniture soon became famous for its perfect balance and purity of form. He set out to 'strip old chairs of their ornamentation', focusing instead on their structural beauty.

NANNA DITZEL (Denmark, 1923-2005)
AND JØRGEN DITZEL (1921-1961)

Nanna studied cabinetmaking and then design at the Royal Academy of Fine Arts in Copenhagen. In 1944, she met Jørgen (whom she later married), who had trained as an upholsterer, and together they opened a design studio in Hellerup. In 1956, they published a book called *Danish Chairs*, which won the Lunning Prize. This enabled them to travel, after which they returned home with new impetus: creating the famous wickerwork armchair in the form of an egg, and also a series of furnishings for children - a high chair and the Toadstool stool - which are still in production today. After Jørgen's death in 1961, Nanna continued to create pieces for children, as well as design jewelry.

POUL KJAERHOLM (Denmark, 1929–1980)

Initially a carpenter, Kjaerholm went on to study cabinetmaking at the Copenhagen School of Arts and Crafts until 1951. His final examination project was the PK24 chaise longue, which was immediately bought and manufactured by Kold Christensen. Next he designed the celebrated PKO chair in moulded plywood, which, though somewhat removed from his pieces with metal and steel legs, is still iconic. He was awarded the Lunning Prize for his furniture, and since the 1980s Fritz Hansen has made and distributed the chairs that he designed in the 1970s.

↖ **Nanna Ditzel** • Bench for Two • Model No. 2600 • Made by Fredericia Furniture • 1989

↑ **Nanna Ditzel** • Toadstool stools • Made by Kold • 1962

↗ **Nanna Ditzel** • Toadstool stools • Made by Trip Trap • 2016

← **Poul Kjaerholm** • PKO • Made by Fritz Hansen • 1952

VERNER PANTON (Denmark, 1926–1998)

Panton graduated in 1951 with a degree in architecture from the Royal Academy of Fine Arts in Copenhagen. After spending a few years working as a member of Arne Jacobsen's team of designers, he opened his own studio in 1955; and then launched a succession of highly original architectural, textile and furniture projects. In 1958, he designed the famous Cone chair, in the shape of an ice cream cone. This iconic design brought him international recognition, and he went on to attract attention with his installations and stage sets, one of which included an exhibition in which he covered a ceiling with carpet and fixed to it his furniture, upside down.

His redesign of the Astoria Restaurant in Trondheim initially caused quite a stir, but eventually proved to be a success. His style of sculptural forms and vibrant colours revolutionized Scandinavian design in the 1960s. Throughout this period he worked incessantly on the project that was closest to his heart: an S-shaped cantilever chair in a single block, the celebrated S-Chair. His first attempt was manufactured by Thonet, but it was not very successful. Next he approached

↑ **Verner Panton** • Cone chair and stool • Panton chair • Both made by Vitra • 1958

Herman Miller, but Miller abandoned the project, in which he had little faith. In the end it was Vitra that produced the first series of the S-Chair in 1967: one hundred chairs in total. In 1979 production was halted, since the material in which the chair was made - plastic - was found to be insufficiently durable. In the 1990s, however, the manufacture of the chair resumed, this time in rigid polyurethane foam.

Panton designed chairs and lamps, together with fabrics and carpets, both in colour and black and white, and in surreal forms, many of which were made by Fritz Hansen. He also designed lamps for Louis Poulsen. Throughout his career, Panton created products that were original and revolutionary. Regarded as a true visionary, he always remained a step ahead of traditional Scandinavian design.

↑ **Eero Aarnio** • Bubble chair • Made by Asko • 1968

EERO AARNIO (Finland, 1932–)

Eero Aarnio is one of a handful of Finnish designers who rose to prominence in the 1960s. He opened his own studio in 1962, with numerous commissions for interior design. Initially he worked with natural materials such as wood and wicker, but quickly turned to new technologies, and was particularly fond of using fibreglass and Plexiglass. His fame rests mainly on his Ball chair (or Globe chair), which he created in 1963.

STEEN ØSTERGAARD
(Denmark, 1935–)

After training to be a joiner, Østergaard spent several years working with Finn Juhl before opening his own studio in 1965. Soon after, he designed his first plastic chair, Cado 290, an ergonomic cantilever chair in a single block. Throughout his career he used plastic in all of his designs.

YRJÖ KUKKAPURO (Finland, 1933–)

Kukkapuro studied architecture at the Helsinki School of Fine Arts and Design, graduating in 1958 and going on to open his own design studio. It was not long before he was dreaming of making chairs in fibreglass and plastic, which was a difficult task in Finland in the 1950s. After a number of experiments, he finally perfected the Karuselli chair, whose form follows the shape of his own body when seated. These were the beginnings of ergonomics in the world of design. He also studied anthropometry (the measurement of the size and proportions of the human body), which he applied to his designs in the aim of making them as close in shape to the human form as possible. One example is his office chair, Fysio.

↑ **Eero Aarnio** • Ball chair • Made by Asko • 1962

TEX·TILES

LIS AHLMANN (Denmark, 1894–1979)

After studying painting, Ahlmann turned her attention to weaving. This was the medium in which she could give full expression to her talents, in a style that was warm and characteristically Nordic. She worked independently, and collaborated with numerous Danish designers, such as Børge Mogensen, producing textiles to accompany their furniture. She had no difficulty transferring her ideas into mass production.

VIBEKE KLINT (Denmark, 1927–)

Klint studied weaving at the School of Applied Arts in Copenhagen, from which she graduated in 1949. She continued her training in France at the École de tapisserie à Aubusson. Her work is very individual, both in terms of her colour palette - red, ochre and black - and in the graphic, geometric design of her fabrics. Her style, drawing on traditional techniques and materials, mark her out as an exceptional weaver.

MAIJA ISOLA (Finland, 1927–2001)

After studying at the School of Fine Arts and Design in Helskinki, Isola joined the firm of Printex, for which she designed numerous prints to be used in furniture. In 1951, Marimekko was set up as a sister branch of the company, with the view to promoting its textiles in the field of interior decoration. Isola's prints were much admired for their originality, their graphic forms and their abstract patterns. During the 1950s, she began to use floral motifs in bright colours, and in the 1960s she had a great deal of success with various series - Melon, Unikko and Kaivo - which have had a major influence on textile design and are still in production today. Her work was the true face of Marimekko.

↑ **Vibeke Klint** • Istra sofa • Made by Boconcept • 2012

OBJECTS · & LAMPS

BING & GRØNDAHL (Denmark, 1853)

The company was formed in 1853 by the sculptor Frederik Grøndahl and the Bing brothers, who were art dealers. They wanted to create a small porcelain factory to produce figurines and other *objets d'art*.

After the Second World War, the company began to make modern tableware, working with a number of different designers. In 1987 it was taken over by Royal Copenhagen, and has continued to maintain a reputation for its high-quality and contemporary products.

← **Aino Aalto** · Bölgeblick glasses · Made by Iittala • 1932

AINO AALTO (Finland, 1894–1949)

Aino graduated in architecture in 1920, and in 1924 she met and married the architect Alvar Aalto. They spent the rest of their lives working together. Aino specialized in designing glassware, much of which was manufactured by Iittala. She designed - in moulded ribbed glass - the Bölgeblick range for them, which included dishes, glasses, jugs and so on. She also designed furniture, an area in which she helped to pioneer the technique of bending plywood.

55

WILHELM KÄGE (Sweden, 1889–1960)

After completing his studies at the Technical School in Stockholm, Käge was employed in 1917 by Gustavsberg, the well-known manufacturer of Swedish porcelain. It was here that he created the renowned *Arbeiterservis* (workers' dinner service) - decorated with blue lilies, it had the prime virtue of being very affordable. In 1933, he designed the Praktika service - comprising modern, stackable white crockery - but this was only moderately successful, since it was a little too austere for its intended consumers. He also developed a complete range 'from the oven to the table' in the same style. Like many of his colleagues, he also created a number of superb, one-off ceramic *objets d'art*.

POUL HENNINGSEN (Denmark, 1894–1967)

Henningsen was one of the great Scandinavian lamp designers. After studying architecture in Copenhagen, he became an art critic, and then co-editor-in-chief for the arts magazine *Klingen*. At the same time he was designing lamps, with a particular interest in the use of materials such as copper and glass. In 1924, shortly after finishing up the design of a variety of lampposts throughout the city, he created a series of table lamps. Unique for their ability to reduce the glare from the bulbs, they marked the early phase of his famous PH series, including the Artichoke, which are still being manufactured by the family firm of Louis Poulsen. More than any other designer, he dreamed of good design being available to all, and was resolutely opposed to elitist pretensions.

GÖRAN HONGELL (Finland, 1902–1973)

Hongell studied decorative art at the Helsinki School of Fine Arts and Design. He then opened a studio for mural decoration and stained glass, and took part in various competitions for glassware. He worked mainly on *objets d'art* until 1937, after which he began making pressed glass for industry. In 1950, he designed the famous Aarne glasses for Karhula, the company of which he had become artistic director; these glasses are still being manufactured today by Iittala. They are 'a compromise between the stemmed glass and the good old-fashioned tumbler'. Hongell is still regarded as one of the pioneers of industrial glassmaking in Finland.

ACTON BJØRN (Denmark, 1910–1992)

Bjørn was an industrial designer during the Second World War, after which he worked in aviation, notably for Boeing. He opened the Industridesign Agency together with Sigvard Bernadotte, and worked with Bang & Olufsen, which sealed his reputation. He was equally at home with plastic and melamine, materials in which he created a variety of kitchen utensils, including his nesting bowls for Rosti.

↑ **Acton Bjørn** • Nesting bowls • Made
by Rosti • 1950

← **Poul Henningsen** • PH Artichoke Lamp
(updated version of the 1927 design) •
Made by Louis Poulsen • 1980

↑ **Folke Arström** • Focus de Luxe cutlery • Made by Gense • 1950

FOLKE ARSTRÖM (Sweden, 1907–1997)

Arström studied art before opening his own graphic design studio. His first commissions were mainly poster designs. In the late 1930s, attracted by metals such as silver and pewter, he began to design objects such as his renowned cocktail shaker, which is a perfect blend of functionality and aestheticism in the best Scandinavian tradition. He went on to make numerous sets of cutlery, including his Focus de Luxe, which offered a fine alternative to silverware and rapidly became popular in the U.S. He was awarded a gold medal at the Milan Triennale in 1951.

SIGVARD BERNADOTTE (Sweden, 1907–2002)

Bernadotte was one of the pioneers of Scandinavian industrial design. In the early 1930s he joined the studio of the silversmith Georg Jensen, and used geometric forms to brilliant effect in his cutlery designs. He then travelled across Europe and the U.S., meeting many industrial designers, and on his return to Scandinavia linked up with Acton Bjørn with whom, in the 1950s, he formed an industrial design company in Copenhagen. Their first project was an office calculator in metal and plastic. They subsequently worked for several companies, designing electrical and electronic goods for the general public.

↑ **Sigvard Bernadotte** · Bernadotte cutlery ·
Made by Georg Jensen • 1939

↑ **Kaj Franck** · Kartio vase ·
Made by Iittala • 1958

KAJ FRANCK (Finland, 1911–1989)

Franck was one of the most prestigious glass and ceramic designers in Finland.
He graduated from the Central School of Applied Arts in Helsinki in 1932 and,
after the war, having gained experience in the field of interior design, he
began work for Arabia. His geometrically shaped crockery sets were in marked
contrast to the aesthetics of the time, which tended to favour curved forms.
In 1950 he was appointed artistic director of the large glassworks Nuutajärvi,
where he became quite prolific in the field of *objets d'art*. He achieved his
aesthetic ideal with the Kilta range in 1952, which was made by Arabia, but at
the same time he designed a great deal of glassware for Iittala, including their
Kartio vases and pitchers. Franck was a typical Scandinavian designer in the
sense that he created functional objects as well as series of limited pieces.
Toward the end of his career, he reworked his Kilta collection, which has now
become the Teema service and is still being manufactured by Littala.

↑ **Henning Koppel** • 'Den Gravide And' pitcher • Made by Georg Jensen • 1951

↗ **Tapio Wirkkala** • Chanterelle vase • Made by Iittala • 1946

↗ **Stig Lindberg** • Pungo vases • Made by Gustavsberg • 1953

TAPIO WIRKKALA (Finland, 1915–1985)

Wirkkala was one of the great Scandinavian designers, whose special talent was his ability to make virtuoso use of any material: glass or ceramics, metal or wood. He was equally brilliant at designing furniture, jewelry, *objets d'art* and lamps. His inspiration was always drawn directly from nature, like the Chanterelle vase of blown glass which he designed in 1946 for Iittala. For a long time he worked for Rosenthal Porcelain, designing magnificent services, vases, cutlery and so on. His glassware, whether *objets d'art* or for every day use, comprised a major part of his work. He invented frosted glass during the 1970s, and also designed many pieces in moulded and textured glass.

STIG LINDBERG (Sweden, 1916–1982)

Lindberg studied design at the Technical School in Stockholm, and subsequently worked in ceramics at the Gustavsberg studios. In 1942, he produced his first collection of painted terracottas, and he also designed glassware and fabrics. He was appointed artistic director of the Gustavsberg Company in the 1950s, and during this time he designed the famous Pungo vase. He continued his career in Italy, where he opened his own design studio.

HENNING KOPPEL (Denmark, 1918–1981)

After studying design and then sculpture, Koppel began his career making silver jewelry. In 1945 he commenced a long and fruitful collaboration with the Georg Jensen company, which specialized in silverware. His work followed the Danish tradition of pure craftsmanship and, as well as jewelry, he created dinner services, cutlery and futuristically shaped and quasi-organic pitchers and carafes.

JENS H. QUISTGAARD (Denmark, 1919-2008)

Quistgard started out making sculptures in wood and, after the Second World War, he set himself up as an independent designer. It was then that he began to experiment with different materials, such as bronze, sandstone and steel, in which he designed all sorts of everyday objects: teapots, candlesticks, dishes and so on. His style - organic and sculptural forms - is instantly recognizable. In 1964, he joined forces with an American businessman to create the company Dansk International Designs. Many of his pieces are still regarded as icons of Danish design, including his famous teak ice bucket.

SAARA HOPEA (Finland, 1925-1984)

First and foremost a ceramist, it was in this capacity that Hopea worked for seven years as a core member of the Arabia Company. During the 1950s she designed the famous No. 1718 stackable glass and the No. 1618 jug for Nuutajärvi. They won silver medals at the 1954 Milan Triennale, and were soon being mass produced. She also developed glassware that was delicately mottled in style.

JACOB JENSEN (Denmark, 1926-2015)

After completing his studies at the Copenhagen School of Arts and Crafts, Jensen worked as a designer at the studio of Sigvard Bernadotte and Acton Bjørn. In 1961, he set up his own design studio, and among his clients were Bang & Olufsen. He is one of Denmark's best known industrial designers, famous for his aluminium hi-fi equipment and for the simple precision of his forms. His son, Timothy, now runs the studio.

→ **Jens H. Quistgaard** • Ice bucket • Made by Dansk • c. 1960

← **Saara Hopea** • Stackable glasses •
Made by Nuutajärvi • 1954

→ **Saara Hopea** • Stackable jug and glasses • Made by Nuutajärvi • 1954

↑ **Erik Magnussen** • Vacuum jugs • Made by Shelton • 1978

ERIK MAGNUSSEN (Denmark, 1940–)

After studying ceramics, Magnussen worked as a designer for Bing & Grøndahl. He was awarded the Lunning Prize for his creations, which included his teapot with integrated strainer. He is best known for the work he has done since 1976 in partnership with the Danish firm of Stelton, which produced a series of steel tableware, such as the Vacuum jug and his celebrated oil and petrol lamps.

TIMO SARPANEVA (Finland, 1926–2006)

Sarpaneva studied at the Helsinki School of Fine Arts and Design, and was then employed by Iittala to organize exhibitions. Subsequently, he worked for a while in the field of textiles, but it was his glassware that brought him to the attention of an international audience. During the 1960s, he designed the renowned series of Finlandia vases for Iittala, with textured glass that imitates tree bark in appearance. Each piece is unique. He also did work for Rosenthal Porcelain and designed for Iittala his celebrated enamelled cast-iron pots with teak handles.

↖ **Timo Sarpaneva** • Cast iron pots • Made by Iittala • 1960

↑ **Poul Christiansen** • Model No. 172 • Made by Le Klint • 1972

LE KLINT (Denmark, 1943)

In 1901, the engineer Peder Vilhelm Jensen-Klint designed an oil lamp with a sandstone base and a lampshade made from folded parchment. A collar protected the paper from the heat so that it was able to filter the light. The family soon began to make all kinds of folded lampshades, and in 1943 one of his sons invented the hanging lamp, following the same principle. That was the moment when they decided to establish the family company Le Klint. This simple lamp, geometric and sculptural, is particularly suited to modern interiors, and the Klint brothers have designed numerous variations of the original lamp, which are always made by hand. They have continued to attract talented designers, and still make lamps in their studios in Denmark.

Arabia

68

Fritz Hansen

68

Artek

70

Iittala

70

Louis Poulsen

70

Marimekko

71

Royal Copenhagen

68

MAKERS AND MANUFACTURERS

ROYAL COPENHAGEN (Denmark, 1775)

Royal Copenhagen was the first porcelain manufacturer to be founded under royal patronage. By the end of the eighteenth century, it had established its reputation with its blue-and-white dinner services. Equally outstanding were its figurines and its high-quality objects in bisque. Experiments with different pigments and glazes ensured continuous creative development, as did a succession of talented designers from around 1870 onward. Since the early twentieth century, the company has had its own integral design department. Now owned by the brewery of Carlsen, Royal Copenhagen remains one of the great Scandinavian companies, and continues to produce iconic designs.

FRITZ HANSEN (Denmark, 1872)

In 1872 the cabinetmaker Fritz Hansen opened a studio in Copenhagen, specializing in woodturning. In 1915, his son, Christian, shifted the company's focus to industrialized mass production, and during the 1920s, it took up the process of woodbending invented by Michael Thonet. By keeping abreast of technological advances, Fritz Hansen continually modernized its products, one of which was the famous Dan chair, which bears a curious resemblance to Thonet's bistrot chair and itself became a landmark in the history of Scandinavian design. In 1952, Arne Jacobsen designed the stackable Myren chair and the remarkable Ant chair for the company. The latter was a real turning point in design history, with its back and seat being made of a single sheet of moulded plywood. This was followed by the Series 7 chair, which is still being produced in various forms: with three legs, four legs and arm rests. It was also Fritz Hansen that manufactured Jacobsen's celebrated Egg and Swan chairs, as well as Verner Panton's 1-2-3 chairs.

Fritz Hansen remains one of Scandinavia's foremost furniture makers, and has played a major role in promoting the pure elegance of Scandinavian furniture all over the world. The name is still synonymous with the combination of form and function that is characteristic of all Scandinavian design.

ARABIA (Finland, 1873)

For almost 150 years, Arabia has been the flag-bearer of Finnish and indeed Scandinavian design, being renowned for its porcelain. Arabia products are instantly recognizable for their timeless beauty, their outstanding quality and their functionality. The first designer to be employed by the company was Thure Öberg, who created numerous vases decorated with floral motifs and female nudes. In 1900, Arabia won a gold medal at the *'Exposition Universelle'* in Paris. From that moment on, the company's international reputation was sealed. Blessed with a number of fine designers, it mass-produced some spectacular pieces, ranging from ceramic art (their crackle-glaze vases) to Kurt Ekholm's Sinivalko, the 'everyday crockery' in blue and white, which went in to production in 1936. This standard of excellence has continued right through to the present, reinforced by its technical expertise and ability to attract the best designers. In 1997, Pia Törnell designed for the company the well-known Tilda bowl range with stackable lids.

→ **Arne Jacobsen** • Egg chair • Made by Fritz Hansen • 1958

LOUIS POULSEN (Denmark, 1874)

This company began life as a small hardware store. The nephew of the proprietor, Louis Poulsen, set up an electrical department which he himself managed. In 1911, Sophus Kaastrup-Olsen, one of the shareholders, joined the company and developed it impressively. The arrival of the designer Poul Henningsen in 1924 resulted in a series of revolutionary PH lamps. At that time, the light emitted from electric bulbs was far too bright, and so he designed a lamp comprising several shades that enabled the glare to be filtered. This was the very embodiment of Scandinavian design, combining functionality and aestheticism, and it was taken up by numerous architects, who incorporated it into their major projects. By 1932, the company had sold 30,000 PH lamps across the world. Later it employed many talented designers, such as Verner Panton and Arne Jacobsen, thus ensuring that it remained at the forefront of contemporary design.

IITTALA (Finland, 1881)

The glassworks Iittala was founded by Petrus Magnus Abrahamsson, master glassblower. Initially, its main product was simple, everyday glassware. However, it quickly established a reputation for high quality and became a benchmark of Finnish design. After serious financial problems it was eventually taken over by the Ahlström Group, which merged the company with the Karhula glassworks. The amalgamation brought major technical advances, and Iittala then focused on *objets d'art* in limited editions. From the 1930s on, it has attracted many outstanding designers, including the Aaltos, Tapio Wirkkala and Kaj Franck, resulting in such splendours as Wirkkala's Chanterelle vase, with its organic forms, and Alvar Aalto's Savoy Vase. In 1990, the company was bought by the Hackman Group, which opened up

international outlets and also facilitated collaboration with foreign designers. Today, Iittala incorporates four brands, one of which is Arabia, and it is still a byword for Scandinavian principles and aestheticism.

ARTEK (Finland, 1935)

Alvar and Aino Aalto joined forces with the patrons and collectors Harry and Maire Gullichsen and Nils-Gustav Hahl in 1935 to create the Artek Company for the sale and distribution of furniture. The Aaltos soon filled a thick catalogue with their stackable chairs and stools, which included the famous L-Leg. Today, Artek continues to distribute their furniture and lamps,

→ **Poul Hennington** • PH lamps • Made by Louis Poulsen • 1958

but it also promotes the work of other designers. Artek remains a model of Scandinavian design *par excellence*, combining the aesthetic with the functional.

MARIMEKKO (Finland, 1951)

The well-known textile factory of Marimekko is in fact a branch of Printex, whose aim was to create original designs for the post-war world of fashion and interior design. Maija Isola was appointed chief designer of the firm and created simple but bold silk-screen prints in cheap cotton materials. Marimekko means 'Marie's dress' - or 'a dress for all occasions' - once again following the ideology of Scandinavian design:

'something beautiful for everyone'. It was not long before various collections of dresses appeared, as unconventional as the prints and materials characteristic of the brand. Since the mid-1960s, Marimekko has also manufactured the fabrics, clothes and accessories of other designers.

INNOVATIVE BRANDS

ERICSSON (Sweden, 1876)

Magnus Ericsson founded the firm of Ericsson in Stockholm in the latter half of the nineteenth century, initially to repair telegraphic equipment. He soon realized that the future would see the evolution of this apparatus, and in 1890 he launched his first domestic model. After a few improvements, he created his 'best-seller' in 1892 - an office telephone with a microphone. In 1930, the company devoted itself mainly to improving the design of its equipment: with the engineer Christian Bjerknes and the artist Jean Heiberg collaborating to produce a telephone made of Bakelite, the DHB 1001. With its curved forms, it was a completely new design, which lasted well into the 1950s. In 1956, Ericsson launched the Ericofon, an innovative telephone all in one piece. It remained a pinnacle of design and technology for many years. In 1970, a version of the Ericofon with keys went on the market and was extremely successful. Then, in the 1980s, Ericsson approached the era of the mobile telephone with the same brilliance as it had shown in its mastery of the office telephone, and the company soon became a leading manufacturer in this field as well. Its

↑ **Ericofon Cobra** • Made by Ericsson • 1970

design continued to be as fresh and original as ever until the first decade of the twenty-first century. Ericsson is one of the world leaders in the field of telecommunication products today. However, this Swedish brand is sometimes now regarded as being a little too conservative.

↑ **Peter Bang** • Hyperbo 5 RG • Made by Bang & Olufsen • 1934

BANG & OLUFSEN (Denmark, 1925)

Bang & Olufsen was founded in 1925 by Peter Bang and Svend Olufsen. Bang had graduated from Aarhus School of Engineering in 1924. Since childhood he had dreamed of inventing a radio that would not need batteries. Svend Olufsen also had a dream: to make a radio that would work off the mains. It was therefore only natural that the two should join forces to form a company. A year later, they had perfected their first electric radio: the Five Lamper. The only black mark against it was its appearance. It was made in wood - walnut and maple - a material that clashed with the modern technology it housed. Stung by such criticism, Bang threw himself into the task of encasing his radio in a properly modern shell. It was only a year later that they produced a radio of pure elegance, the Hyperbo 5 RG, a masterpiece of modern aesthetics in black metal, inspired by the tubular steel chairs of Marcel Breuer. In 1938, they used Bakelite to create an aerodynamic case for their radio.

There is a striking American attitude in their formal approach to design, and in fact Bang spent some time in the U.S., returning full of enthusiasm for their streamlined forms. Bang & Olufsen continued to produce a variety of radios, and during the 1950s were quick to team up with designers such as Acton Bjørn. These collaborations resulted in products of the highest technical and aesthetic quality. The company's avant-garde designs were much sought after, although they were also expensive. Between 1960 and 1980, Jacob Jensen created a number of outstanding models, though always remaining faithful to the characteristic blend of technical and aesthetic excellence. Later, the company diversified into products such as telephones and plasma screens. The name is still synonymous with good design, high quality and originality - essentially Scandinavian.

ELECTROLUX (Sweden, 1919)

The original firm of AB Lux was launched in 1901 with the invention of an external lamp called Lux, and in 1912, the company invented the very first vacuum cleaner. In 1915 it merged with Elektromekanista, and then in 1919 with Svenska Elektron AB to form Electrolux. The company continued to improve their vacuum cleaners, and conceived of the sledge vacuum cleaner. In 1922, they invented a refrigerator, which they produced in limited quantities for AB Arctic, a small company that they took over in 1925. They then vastly increased the manufacture of refrigerators, and later expanded their manufacturing base to England and the U.S.

In the late 1930s, Raymond Loewy became head of the design department, and streamlined elegance became the trademark of the company's products. In 1940, it was Electrolux that produced the first domestic robot, and today it is still noted for home appliances that combine practicality with visual appeal. Electrolux was the first international manufacturer to sell more than fifty million products a year.

SAAB (Sweden, 1937)

Svenska Aeroplan AB was founded by two financiers just before the Second World War. They recruited engineers from Boeing, and made aeroplanes equipped with the very first ejector seats. After the war, they decided to branch out into the motor industry. As the team had specialized in aeronautics, they had no preconceptions, and this resulted in some very original designs for their cars.

In 1949, the Saab 92 was designed to be 'the first small car for the people', in the true ideological tradition of Scandinavian design. The model is outstanding for its attention to detail and its durability.

IKEA (Sweden, 1943)

Ingvar Kamprad founded Ikea in 1943 in Småland, one of the poorest regions in Sweden. His plan was to sell a variety of products by mail order. From the 1950s on, Ikea sold furniture at factory prices, solely via their catalogue. The young entrepreneur felt that design products were too expensive, and inspired by his personal mission of social democratization, he created objects that were practical, beautiful and, above all, cheap.

From the very beginning, the company's ethic was focused on good, democratic design, with the motto being: 'Form, function and affordable prices.' Kamprad recruited talented designers, and one important element of his low-cost strategy lay in the economics of transport. By introducing self-assembly furniture, he considerably lowered the cost of transport and hence the retail price of his products. Another innovative idea is the concept of the modular system: items of furniture that can be adapted to suit the specific interiors and tastes of their buyers. And all this achieved with the aid of flat packs!

In 1958, Ikea opened its first store, in Älmhult. In the last fifty years, the company has always kept up with new trends and technologies, using plywood, plastic, pinewood and so on in its products.

Today, Ikea owns more than 145 stores, is a world leader in its field and has done wonders for Scandinavian design. Ingvar Kamprad's latest challenge? Small, prefabricated houses.

→ **Saab** • Model 92 • 1948

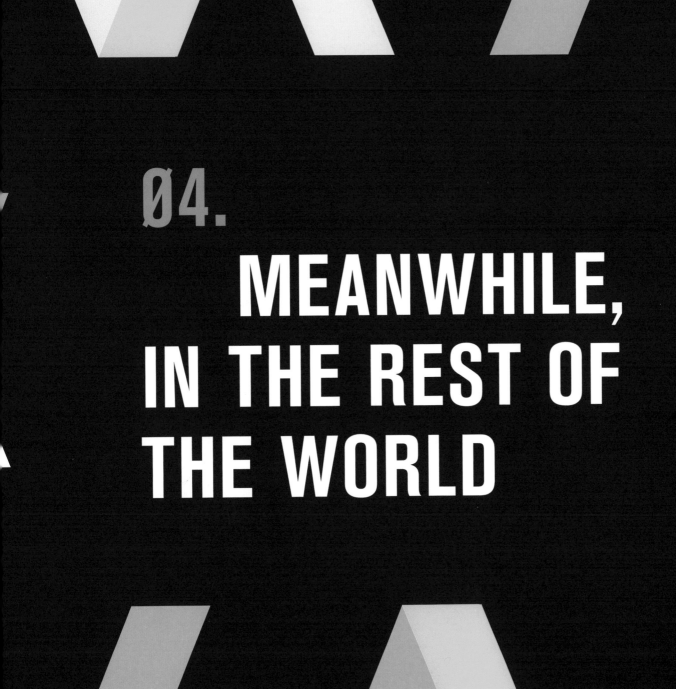

Ø4.

MEANWHILE, IN THE REST OF THE WORLD

Until the early 1900s, Art Nouveau, with its myriad of organic forms, motifs and gilded splendours, reigned supreme in Europe. Then in 1919 the Bauhaus, a school of decorative and industrial arts in Germany, appeared on the scene. This eventually extended its influence all across Europe, mainly in the domains of architecture and design. It expressed a strong desire for change, and signalled the end of Art Nouveau. The basic principles of the movement were purity of form and, above all, 'the disappearance of decoration in everyday objects', according to Adolf Loos, who articulated the aims of the movement in Austria.

Bauhaus ideology lay at the heart of Le Corbusier's work in France, and he put its ideas into architectural practice from 1923 onward.

With the advent of mass production, the challenge now was to find a balance between the criteria of creative aestheticism, mass production and social ideals. The result was pure forms that were more cubic, and perhaps less natural and organic, than the products being produced by Scandinavian designers.

FRANCE

Right up until the 1960s, France was a veritable hotbed of design. The following is a select list of the outstanding designers that rose to prominence during this period.

JACQUES VIÉNOT (1893–1959)

Viénot designed the Institut Français d'Esthétique Industrielle in 1951. Its aim was to improve the design of French industrial products, and to create a true industrial aesthetic. Jean Prouvé was an active participant in the foundation of the institute.

JEAN PROUVÉ (1901–1984)

After serving an apprenticeship in the craft of wrought iron, Prouvé opened his own studio in Nancy in 1924, where, shortly after, he designed his famous reclining chair. Naturally many of his creations were in wrought iron, but much of his furniture was made of folded metal plates, and he also worked in wood. He has collaborated with many of the great architects of his time.

LE CORBUSIER (1887–1965)

Le Corbusier, whose real name was Charles-Édouard Jeanneret-Gris, initially studied engraving in his home country of Switzerland. Trouble with his eyesight prevented him from pursuing this career, so he turned to painting. However, his professor of drawing suggested he should take up architecture instead, which he duly did. After several years travelling around Europe, including a spell in Paris, he returned to Switzerland around 1910 and set himself up as an independent architect. In 1917, he returned to Paris, where he opened his studio, and in 1933 he became a naturalized French citizen. During the 1920s, he designed a series of remarkable villas and residential blocks, revolutionizing architecture with his purist style, epitomized by the famous Villa Savoye. At the same time, he experimented with materials and forms in his furniture, pursuing his ideas to their logical conclusion. He created many iconic designs, such as the LC4 chaise longue and the LC1 chair. Le Corbusier may be said to have laid the foundations of modern architecture, with its simplicity of form and its austere discipline: 'Where there is order there is wellbeing.'

↑ **Jean Prouvé** • Standard chairs • Made by Vitra • 1934

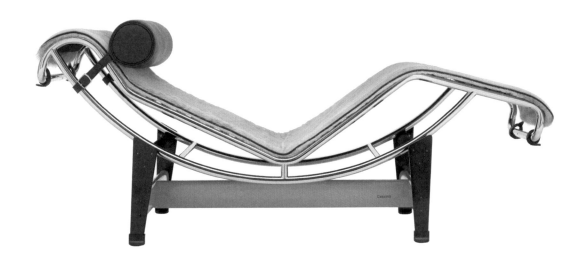

↑ **Le Corbusier, Charlotte Perriand and Pierre Jeanneret** •
LC4 chaise longue • Made by Cassina-Maestri • 1928

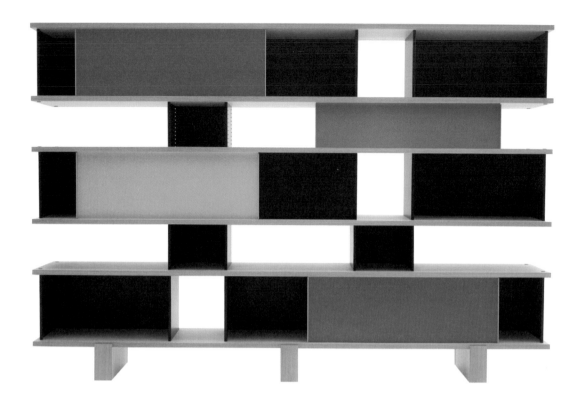

↑ Charlotte Perriand
• Nuage bookcase
• Made by Cassina-Maestri • 1928

CHARLOTTE PERRIAND (1903-1999)

After graduating in the decorative arts in 1935, Perriand worked as an independent designer, notably with Le Corbusier and his cousin Pierre Jeanneret and with Jean Prouvé in Nancy. Her style underwent a radical change after she spent two years in the Far East. These were her 'Japan' years. Her designs, such as her Nuage bookcase, were formally simple but full of colour. This piece is still being produced today by Cassini.

PIERRE GUARICHE (1926-1995)

After studying at the École nationale supérieure des arts décoratifs in Paris, Guariche began his career as an interior decorator and designer, working together with Marcel Gascoin. He is known for the simple elegance of his furniture, which was both modern and affordable. In 2014, Maison du Monde revived thirteen of his most typical designs - proof that his work is as timeless as ever.

SERGE MOUILLE (1922-1988)

After fourteen years at the École des arts appliqués in Paris, Serge Mouille specialized in metalwork and opened his own studio in 1945, where he designed table silverware. In 1953, he designed and made his renowned series of lamps, which in large part were inspired by the female form. Each piece was unique and specifically adapted to the space it was intended to illuminate.

PIERRE PAULIN (1927-2009)

Pierre Paulin learned his craft working
with Marcel Gascoin, and he soon began
to experiment on his own with different
materials, forms and colours. His very
pure style, incorporating organic shapes,
was largely inspired by Scandinavian
design. He created many iconic chairs
that were made of wood and covered in
jersey, such as the Mushroom, the Tulip
and the Ribbon.

↑ **Pierre Guariche** • Guariche chair • Made by Steiner • 1955

← **Serge Mouille** • Standing lamps, single and triple •
Made by Serge Mouille • 1953

01.

02.

03.

04.

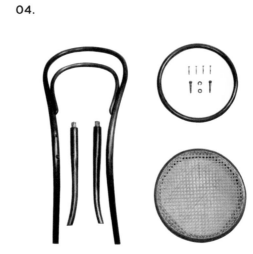

01. Eames • Lounge chair • Made by Vitra • 1956

02. Eames • RAR chairs • Made by Vitra • 1950

03–05. Michael Thonet • Thonet chair No. 14 • Made by Thonet • 1859

GERMANY

In Germany, too, the artistic scene was very lively, and there was a good deal of interaction with Scandinavian designers. The Ulm School of Design was founded in 1953, with the aim of reviving the Bauhaus, which the Nazis had shut down in 1933. This college was an intellectual powerhouse and made a major contribution to the development of design worldwide.

Many Scandinavian designers collaborated with the Thonet Company - founded by Michael Thonet - who had trained as a cabinetmaker. He pioneered the process of bending wood, which was very widely used in Nordic furniture. His iconic chair No. 14, regarded as the prototype bistro chair, was designed in 1859.

THE UNITED STATES

The U.S. was by no means left behind in the quest for modern design. The west coast in particular was a creative hub with its avant-garde villas in locations such as Los Angeles and Palm Springs. Charles and Ray Eames, in particular, are regarded as iconic designers. Charles (1907-1978) opened his architecture studio in St Louis in 1930. As a professor of industrial design, he met and later married Ray (1912-1988), who was his student. They went to Venice, California, and set up a studio for design and interior decoration, where they experimented with moulding and plywood in their furniture designs. They are still famed for their prefabricated Case Study Houses and, of course, their chairs and other furniture, which were made by the Herman Miller Company. Some of the Eames's creations are still being manufactured by Herman Miller in America and Vitra in Switzerland.

Ø5. THE KEY ELEMENTS OF SCANDINAVIAN DESIGN

01.

02.

01. Knudsen Berg Hindenes & Myhr • Plank sofa • Made by DK3 • 2013

02. Børge Mogensen • Shaker furniture • Made by R. Wengler • 1944

03. Nanna Ditzel • Hanging chair • Made by R. Wengler • 1957

03.

1. WOOD, WOOD AND MORE WOOD

Scandinavian designers are champions of natural resources, especially wood. This material is used in all its forms: untreated or polished, painted, light or dark, with teak or pine being the most popular choice. Wood is of course used in the making of furniture, but also in decorative objects, sculptures, accessories and tableware.

↑ **Arne Jacobsen** • Ant chair • Made by Fritz Hansen • 1952

↑ Interior styled by Vitra • 2015

2. WHITE, BLACK AND LIGHT PASTELS

The Scandinavian colour palette is minimalist, with white being the favoured colour for interiors, even down to flooring, which is often painted in this colour. White has the advantage of reflecting light, which is particularly useful in winter, when natural light is scarce. Black offers a visual balance.

Colour is then injected to brighten things up - with pastel shades being most popular. Powder pink, almond green, sky blue and mustard yellow are often harmonized, as are all shades of grey: grey green, grey blue, beige, all the way to khaki.

3. GEOMETRIC

PATTERNS AND GRAPHIC PRINTS

Add a touch of graphic art to your interior with accessories such as cushions, lampshades and blankets. Mixing patterns, especially with textiles, can be particularly striking; adorn your sofa with a collection of cushions, or drape over it black-and-white patterned blankets. The great advantage of using graphic prints and geometric patterns is that you can alter the style of your interiors without having to change your furniture.

You can also add a graphic look to your walls, with wallpaper, pictures or posters, as well as by displaying crockery and decorative items such as vases.

In short, geometry rules - but in small doses!

4. ANIMAL SKINS

Sheepskin is frequently used in Scandinavian interiors, since it adds a touch of warmth to what are typically quite bare and minimalist spaces. It can be used as a rug, draped over a sofa or armchair or made into cushions. Goatskin is also common; it is less soft, but its close-cropped roughness is perhaps more to the modern taste.

5. A SIGNATURE PIECE

This slim, low sideboard is typical of Scandinavian design. Made of wood, it can be placed anywhere without ever taking up too much space precisely because it is long, slim and low. You can put your knick-knacks and *objets d'art* on the top, and an assortment of pictures on the wall above.

Ø6.
CHOOSING YOUR FURNITURE

HOW TO RECOGNIZE SCANDINAVIAN FURNITURE

1. THE MATERIAL IS WOOD: OAK, MAHOGANY, PINE OR TEAK.

The finish is rarely rough, and usually polished or stained. The wood is usually veneered, as can be seen in chairs such as the Ant chair, or comprises a single sheet.

2. THE COMPLEMENTARY MATERIALS ARE USUALLY NATURAL.

The materials most often combined with wood are leather and wicker (in chair seats for example) or cotton or wool.

A combination of teak and imitation leather can often be seen in chairs and armchairs.

3. SHAPES ARE VERY RESTRAINED, WITH FEW DECORATIVE FEATURES.

4. THREE-LEGGED PIECES ARE TYPICAL. Many stools and tables adopt this form.

5. CANTILEVERED FORMS OF SEATING ARE VERY LIKELY TO BE OF SCANDINAVIAN ORIGIN.

6. ANY STRUCTURE IN TUBULAR STEEL CONNECTED TO A SEAT IN LEATHER OR WOOD MAY WELL BE SCANDINAVIAN.

7. LEGS ARE NEARLY ALWAYS SLENDER AND TAPERED WHEN MADE IN WOOD. They may also be made in metal - generally tubular in shape.

8. COMPASS LEGS ARE A TYPICAL FEATURE.

9. WICKER AND RATTAN ARE VERY COMMON IN SMALLER ITEMS OF FURNITURE (SUCH AS COTS AND MIRRORS). They are generally stained and rarely left in their natural state.

10. THE LONG, LOW SIDEBOARD IS A SIGNATURE PIECE. The round or elongated handles are usually integrated into the wood, although sometimes they may have small metal knobs.

On bedside cabinets and chests of drawers, however, the handles are often made in the form of a metal 'U'.

↓ **Arne Jacobsen** • Grand Prix chair • Made by Fritz Hansen • 1960

USEFUL ADDRESSES

Below you will find the addresses of shops and Internet sites that sell Scandinavian furniture and accessories.

SHOPS

Aram
110 Drury Lane
Covent Garden
London WC2B 5SG

Béton Brut
Unit 2, 30 Felstead Street
London E9 5LG

Chase & Sorensen
238B Dalston Lane
London E8 1LQ

Førest London
115 Clerkenwell Road
London EC1R 5BY

The Modern Warehouse
3 Trafalgar Mews
London E9 5JU

Skandium
86 Marylebone High Street
London W1U 4QS

twentytwentyone
274/275 Upper Street
London N1 2UA

INTERNET

www.ebay.co.uk
eBay is a great resource for vintage pieces, which can often be purchased at a fraction of the price of new products. For best results type into the search engine 'Scandinavian design', the product or the designer's name.

www.arabia.fi

www.artek.fi

abelsloane1934.com

www.iittala.com

www.ikea.com

marimekko.com

www.vitra.com

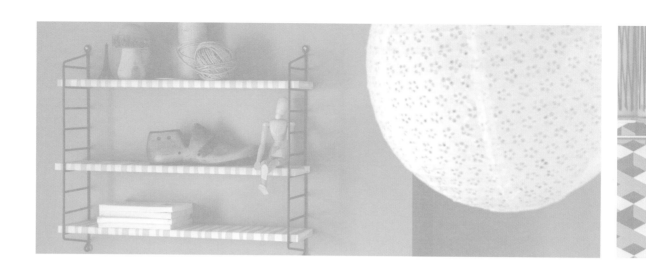

PRACTICAL

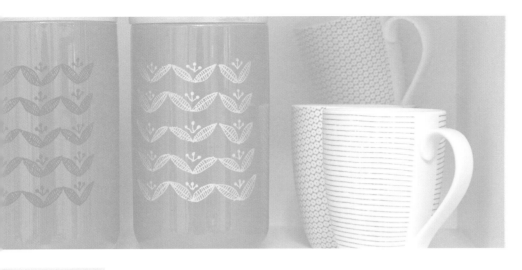

PROJECTS

FURNITURE

EMBROIDER
AN UPHOLSTERED CHAIR

MATERIALS:
upholstered chair + pencil + dressmaker's carbon paper + sticky tape + cotton thread + sewing needle

1. **CHOOSE YOUR CHAIR:** Find a chair that is upholstered in fabric, not imitation leather, and which has compass legs. You can buy one at a cost of between £40 and £130, depending on the condition, sometimes more if it is a recognized brand. If you like the structure of the chair but not the cover, don't worry, it can easily be re-upholstered in fabric of your choice before you start embroidering (see 'Revamp a 1950s chair'; pages 112-13).

2. **PREPARE THE CHAIR:** Vacuum clean the fabric and clean the legs with a soft damp cloth. Once dry, apply antique polish and buff with a clean shoe brush.

3. **TRACE THE PATTERN:** Transfer the flower pattern (fig. 1, page 176) onto the back rest with a pencil and the carbon paper.

4. **START EMBROIDERING:** Separate the cotton thread into three strands, retaining two for the embroidery. Thread the needle and knot at the end. Use running stitch (fig. 20, page 190) to sew the pattern. Take care to keep the stitches and the spaces in-between them consistent in length.

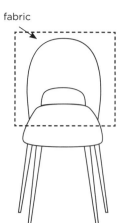

• fig. 1 •

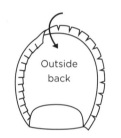

Outside back

• fig. 2 •

• fig. 3 •

• fig. 4 •

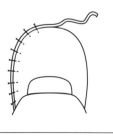

• fig. 5 •

REVAMP A 1950S CHAIR

MATERIALS:
1950s chair + khaki cotton upholstery fabric (3 × 2.3 m) + fabric spray adhesive + wall stapler + yellow piping (2 m in length) + sewing pins + sewing needle + assorted cotton threads

1. **CHOOSE YOUR CHAIR:** Items such as this Pierre Guariche barrel-style chair were very popular in the 1950s. They can be easily sourced online or in shops that stock vintage furniture. They will often be covered in imitation leather, and have compass legs of metal or wood. You can expect to pay between £20 and £40 for such a chair in reasonable condition. Don't worry if the imitation leather is damaged – it won't be visible once the chair has been re-upholstered.

   If you see another style of chair that you prefer, don't hesitate to buy it: the technique of re-upholstering will be the same.

2. **PREPARE THE CHAIR:** Clean the imitation leather and the legs with soap and warm water, removing any grease with a cloth and some stain remover.

3. **START COVERING:** This is a three-stage process: starting with the back rest, then the outside back and finally the seat. Cut a generous-sized rectangle for the back rest; estimate the size by holding the material up against the chair (fig. 1). Allow for a 10-cm overlap, which will be fixed to the outside back, and 7 cm for the internal join. Spray the adhesive on the back rest, position the fabric on top and press firmly to secure. For a close-fitting finish pull the fabric tightly across the surface, following the direction of the weave. Now cut away the excess material. Cut 7-cm-wide notches in the overlap, apply adhesive, and pull tightly onto the outside back (fig. 2). Repeat with the hole at the bottom. Use a knitting needle (or screwdriver) to push the fabric into the internal joins, ensuring that there are no folds or creases.

Repeat this method for the outside back. Cut a large rectangle of fabric. Cut away the excess material, leaving a return of 10 cm. Cut 7-cm notches in the return and fold under before sticking to the back of the chair with the adhesive (fig. 3). When you reach the underside of the seat, turn the fabric under by just 1 cm and pull firmly, using the stapler to fix in place (fig. 4). Position the yellow piping along the top of the back to hide the join, pin down to secure (fig. 5), and sew to fix in place.

Repeat this process for the hole at the bottom, this time sewing together the front and back sections without the piping.

To cover the seat, cut a generous-sized piece of fabric, estimating the size required as before. Apply adhesive to the seat, position the fabric on top and pull hard to avoid creases. Cut away the excess material, retaining a margin of 10 cm. Use a knitting needle to push the fabric into the internal joins. Turn the chair upside down, turn the fabric under by 1 cm and pull tight on to the underside, using the stapler to fix into place as before.

BRIGHTEN UP
A BEDSIDE TABLE

MATERIALS:
bedside table + sandpaper + highly adhesive undercoat + small roller + paintbrush + interior wood paint (in a choice of four colours) + paper + pencil + masking tape

RANGE OF COLOURS ILLUSTRATED:
grey (Down Pipe), black (Off Black), blue (Stiffkey Blue), almond green (Teresa's Green)

1. **CHOOSE YOUR BEDSIDE TABLE:** Find a Scandinavian-style table with compass legs. Don't worry if the veneer is in poor condition - it will be repainted. You can buy tables such as the one illustrated for around £35-70.

2. **PREPARE THE TABLE:** Clean the table with a cloth and some stain remover to remove any grease, and sand to even out the surface. Use a damp cloth to remove any dust that remains, allow to dry. If the table has a handle, remove it before you start painting.

3. **PAINT THE TABLE:** Apply a layer of undercoat paint with a roller (you can use the paintbrush for any difficult to reach areas). Leave to dry for 12 hours (or however long the instructions on the tin recommend).

   Decide on the different colour sections for your table: in the example illustrated the top and the drawer have been painted black, the main body blue and the legs grey. Apply two to three coats of paint to each area, leaving sufficient drying time between layers. Leave to dry for 24 hours. Tip: if your table has a drawer, you can remove it and paint separately.

   Next paint the triangles on top (almond green has been used in the table illustrated). Make a triangle template (fig. 2, page 177). Position the template in each corner and trace around it with a pencil. Apply two to three layers of your chosen colour to the areas marked (leaving sufficient drying time between each). Tip: you can use masking tape to achieve a neat finish. Remove the tape when you have finished the last coat so that it doesn't stick to the paint as it dries.

DECORATE STRING SHELVING

MATERIALS:
2 String shelving panels + shelves (1.5 cm thick) + vintage wallpaper + wallpaper glue + brush with large bristles + Stanley knife

1. **CHOOSE YOUR STRING SUPPORTS AND SHELVES:** A 1950s design classic conceived by the Swedish designer and architect Nils Strinner, String shelving is practical, flexible and timeless. You will save money if you purchase the panels and shelves separately rather than as a unit, and have the latter cut to fit. The panels cost approximately £40-100 each, depending on the size.

2. **CUT THE BOARDS:** If buying the shelves separately, cut to the dimensions you require, retaining approximately 2-2.5 cm to project beyond the panels. Alternatively you could order them to size from a specialist retailer (check online for stockists).

3. **APPLY THE WALLPAPER:** Clean the shelves with a damp cloth to remove any dust. Next cut the paper to the dimensions required using the formula below, and fig. 4, page 177, as a guide:

   Length of paper = 1 × shelf length + 2 × 1.5 cm (the shelf thickness)

   Width of paper = 2 × shelf width + 2 × 1.5 cm (the shelf thickness) + 5 cm overlap

Spread the glue evenly over one side of the first shelf and carefully position it centrally on the wallpaper. Next, apply glue to the shelf ends and the underside. Pull the width of the paper up from the bottom and smooth it over the upper side of the shelf, first from one edge, then the other.

With the Stanley knife cut four triangular notches, one in each corner, into the overlap at each end so that there are four paper 'tabs' either end. Apply a layer of glue to the underside of each long tab. Press the side tabs down first, then the one at the bottom, and finally the one at the top (this process is rather like wrapping a present). Repeat for the remaining shelves.

REPAINT A CHILD'S RATTAN CHAIR AND KNIT A SEAT

MATERIALS:

For the chair: a child's rattan chair + highly adhesive undercoat + interior wood paint (grey or another colour of your choice) + paintbrush

For the seat: 1 ball of bulky pale pink yarn + 6.5-mm knitting needles

1. **CHOOSE YOUR CHAIR:** Small, 1950s rattan chairs are readily available, both online and in vintage shops, at a cost of roughly between £40 and £80, depending on the condition.

2. **PREPARE THE CHAIR:** Clean the rattan with a cloth and some stain remover to remove any grease.

3. **START PAINTING:** Apply a layer of undercoat, taking care not to miss the areas in-between and under the weave. Remember to rotate the chair while you are painting so that it is completely covered. Allow 12 hours to dry (or however long the instructions on the tin recommend).

   Next, apply two layers of grey paint, waiting at least four hours between applications (again refer to the instructions on the tin).

4. **KNIT THE SEAT:**

   Cast on 20 stitches.

   Row 1: purl 20 stitches
   Row 2: repeat
   Row 3: purl 1, increase 1, purl 18, increase 1, purl 1
   Row 4: purl 22
   Row 5: purl 1, increase 1, purl 20, increase 1, purl 1
   Rows 6-18: purl 24
   Row 19: decrease 1, purl 20, decrease 1
   Row 20: purl 22
   Row 21: decrease 1, purl 18, decrease 1
   Row 22: purl 20
   Row 23: repeat
   Cast off

CUSTOMIZE A SIDE TABLE

MATERIALS:
coffee table or side table + sandpaper + highly adhesive undercoat + small roller + paintbrush + ruler + pencil + wood paint (in a choice of four colours) optional: masking paper + Stanley knife + spray mount

RANGE OF COLOURS ILLUSTRATED:
greyish-beige (Lamp Room Grey), ecru (Skimming Stone), pale pink (Nancy's Blushes), almond green (Teresa's Green)

1. **CHOOSE YOUR TABLE:** Find a Scandinavian-style table with compass legs. Don't worry if the veneer is damaged or the polish scratched - it is going to be repainted. Such tables are reasonably priced, costing between £40 and £100.

2. **PREPARE THE TABLE:** Wipe the table with a cloth and some stain remover to remove any grease. Sand for an even surface. Wipe with a damp cloth to remove any remaining varnish and leave to dry. If there are any holes in the veneer, they can be filled with wood filler. Allow the filler to dry and sand over the holes before painting.

3. **START PAINTING:** Apply the undercoat with a roller. You can use a paintbrush for any difficult to reach areas. Leave to dry for 12 hours (or however long the instructions on the tin recommend). Apply two to three coats of your base colour (in the table illustrated, greyish-beige has been used), allowing sufficient drying time between each. Leave to dry for 24 hours.

4. **DECORATE THE TABLE:** Mark out the pattern (fig. 5, page 177; this template fits a table measuring 64 × 42 cm, with each rectangle measuring 4 × 21 cm) on the top of the table. Next make a colour guide (fig. 5) so that each colour is evenly distributed across the top. Be careful, you can easily go wrong!

Tip: You could use masking paper while painting. Cut the paper into three sheets, one for each colour (remember you won't need one for the base colour). Transfer the pattern on to the paper and cut out the triangles for colour 2 using a ruler and Stanley knife. Apply a thin layer of spray mount to the paper and position it on top of the table. Press down firmly then apply with a roller two to three coats. Remove and leave to dry. Clean the table top so that there is no residue of the spray mount, and repeat the process with the triangles for colours 3 and 4. You could also use masking tape to mask out the areas, apply the paint and remove the tape before the last coat has dried.

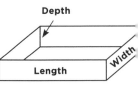

Depth

Length

Width

• fig. 1 •

39 cm

27 cm

• fig. 2 •

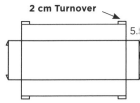

2 cm Turnover

5.

• fig. 3 •

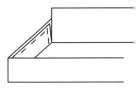

• fig. 4 •

LINE THE DRAWERS OF A WORK TABLE

MATERIALS:
small Scandinavian worktable with drawers + printed fabric + iron + strong spray adhesive + assorted braids + wall stapler + fabric glue

1. **CHOOSE YOUR TABLE:** Choose a typically Scandinavian table - one made in light polished wood, and with metal or wooden compass legs is ideal. You can buy one for around £100, although be prepared to pay more for a signature piece. Or find a small chest of drawers, which will cost around £140-200.

2. **PREPARE THE TABLE:** Rub down the wooden legs with a soft cloth and some antique polish. Vacuum clean the inside of the drawers.

3. **LINE THE DRAWERS:** Measure each drawer - width, length and depth - to determine the size of fabric you will need, remembering to add a 2-cm turnover at all edges. You can use the following formula as a guide:

   Fabric length: drawer length + 2 × depth + 2 × 2 cm (the turnover).

   Fabric width: drawer width + 2 × depth + 2 × 2 cm (the turnover).

   So, for example, in the drawer illustrated, which is 39 × 27 cm, 5.5 cm in depth:

   Length: 39 + 2 × 5.5 + 2 × 2 = 54 cm
   Width: 27 + 2 × 5.5 + 2 × 2 = 42 cm

You should, therefore, cut a 54 × 42-cm rectangle for the lining of your drawer.

Carefully mark the position of the drawer's interior corners on the fabric. Then cut from each corner of the fabric to a point 0.5 cm from the drawer corner. To reduce overlap, trim away the fabric in a V shape at each corner, either side of your cut, making sure to leave a 2-cm turnover (fig. 2).

Before positioning the fabric, fold the 2-cm turnover to the wrong side and iron flat (fig. 3). Fold and iron the lines of the drawer's inner edges. Apply spray adhesive to the drawer and lay the fabric inside, making sure that it fits neatly into the corners. Press the fabric firmly into place, taking care to smooth out any creases: start at the centre and work your way out to the sides. Once secure, staple the fabric at 5-cm intervals, 5 mm down from the upper edge. Repeat at the corners, again inserting staples 5 mm from the join (fig. 4).

4. **ADD THE BRAID:** Measure the length of the braid you need: 2 × length + 2 × width + 1 cm overlap. Apply glue to the braid and position on top of the upper staples.

REJUVENATE
A CHAIR WITH COLOUR

MATERIALS:
chair + sandpaper + highly adhesive undercoat + small roller + paintbrush + interior wood paint (in a choice of two colours) + masking tape

1. **CHOOSE A CHAIR:** Find a chair that is Scandinavian in style. The one illustrated is available from the retailer Alinea at a cost of £40. There are plenty of attractive and reasonably price models available from most large furniture stores.

2. **PREPARE THE CHAIR:** Wipe with a cloth and some stain remover to remove any grease. Sand and use a damp cloth to remove any remaining varnish. Leave to dry.

3. **START PAINTING:** Apply the undercoat with the roller, using a paintbrush for any difficult to reach areas, then leave to dry for 12 hours (or however long the instructions on the tin recommend). Apply two to three coats of the base colour with a paintbrush (marron glacé was used in the chair illustrated) allowing sufficient drying time between each. Leave to dry for 12 hours. Mark off the area you wish to paint in your second colour (here pale pink), making a horizontal line with a pencil and ruler across the struts, 20 cm from the top. Repeat with the legs, 15 cm up from the bottom. Wrap masking tape around each strut and leg, taking care to ensure that it is perfectly horizontal. With the paintbrush apply three coats of pink paint, allowing sufficient drying time between each. Once you have finished your last coat, remove the masking tape quickly and carefully, to prevent it from sticking to the drying paint.

ACCESSORIES

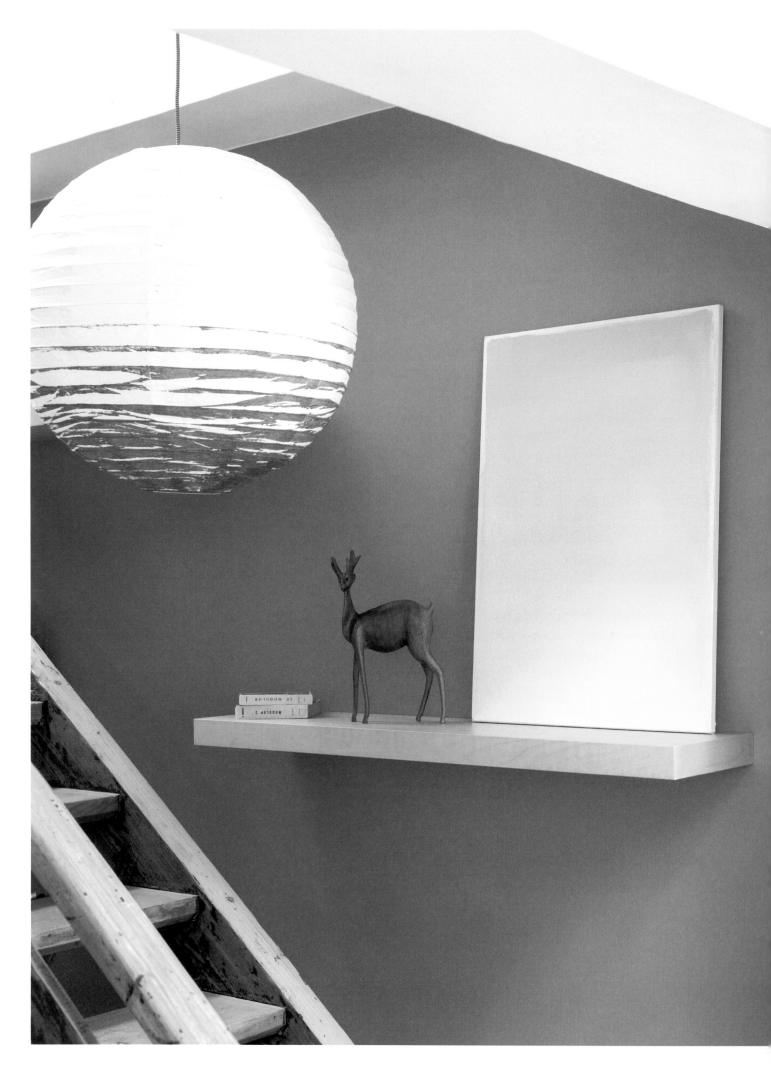

CREATE A GRADATION PAINTING AND CUSTOMIZE A CHINESE LANTERN

MATERIALS:

For the painting: pre-stretched canvas (approx. 70 × 50 cm) + pale pink and white water-based paint (such as acrylic or house paint) + paintbrush with large bristles

For the lamp: Chinese lantern + small roller + grey water-based paint

1. **FOR THE PAINTING:** Squeeze the paint onto a plate, taking care to keep the two colours separate. Moisten the brush with water. Starting at the top of the canvas, work from left to right, and apply the pink, in a strip roughly 4 cm high. Moisten the brush again and add a strip of white paint. Run the brush across the join until the colours blend together seamlessly. Continue in this manner, each time adding more white, until you have reached the bottom of the canvas. The final strip should be only white. Tip: moistening your brush in-between applications will help the colours to blend together better. Tip: Remember to leave a border of 1 cm around the canvas (do not paint right to the edges).

2. **FOR THE LAMP:** With the lantern still flat, bottom side up, take the roller and apply the paint. Gently open up the lantern. This is the moment of discovery, when the random pattern that you have created is suddenly revealed. Each lantern you make in this way will be unique!

   Next insert the metal holders, taking care not to pierce the paper. Hang the lantern up to dry.

MAKE SILHOUETTE PRINTS
OF ICONIC DESIGNS

MATERIALS:
6 sheets of sky-blue Canson paper (30 × 20 cm) + 3 light oak frames (30 × 20 cm) + printer

1. **FOR THE PRINTS:** Scan and enlarge the silhouettes (figs 6-8, pages 178-80) to the dimensions you require and print onto the sky-blue paper.

2. **FOR THE FRAMES:** Make internal mounts by cutting rectangles (approx. 24 × 18 cm) out of the centre of the remaining sheets of paper. Place a border on top of each printed silhouette and insert into a frame.

ENLIVEN AN INTERIOR WITH SUNBURST MIRRORS

MATERIALS:
selection of rattan mirrors (how many is up to you) + highly adhesive undercoat + wide pointed paintbrush + interior wood paint in several colours + masking tape

RANGE OF COLOURS ILLUSTRATED:
light green (Teresa's Green), grey (Down Pipe), light pink (Nancy's Blushes), khaki green (Olive)

1. **CHOOSE YOUR MIRRORS:** You can find sunburst mirrors in second-hand shops, stores that specialize in 1950s furniture and online (type in 'rattan mirror', 'wicker mirror' or 'sunburst mirror' in your search engine). The benefit of using online retailers is that you can compare several mirrors at a time, which will help you to visualize how they might look as a group. Consider buying mirrors in different sizes, ranging between 30 and 70 cm in diameter (including the frame). They can be bought at a cost of around £20 and £40, depending on the size and condition.

2. **PREPARE THE MIRRORS:** Remove any grease with a cloth and some stain remover. Leave to dry. Position the masking tape on top of the mirror, reaching as far under the rattan or rays as you can. Apply the undercoat and leave to dry.

3. **START PAINTING:** Paint the entire frame, back and front, in your base colour. Apply a second coat when the first has dried. To create a two-tone effect, position the masking tape vertically from one end of the frame to the other and paint one side in the second colour. Once dry, apply a second coat and remove the masking tape.

Position the mirrors on the wall. You could intersperse large mirrors with smaller ones for an eye-catching composition, or hang them next to the pictures or photographs already on display in your home.

MAKE A SCANDINAVIAN-STYLE FRESCO

MATERIALS:
potato + Stanley knife + yellow water-based paint (such as acrylic or house paint) + long spirit level

1. **PREPARE THE WALL AND THE STAMP:** Decide on where you want to paint the fresco, and mark out the area with a pencil. Cut the potato into two, and dispose of one half. Cut the cross motif (fig. 3, page 177) into the potato with a Stanley knife, and remove the excess. Pat with a kitchen towel to remove as much starch as possible.

2. **START PAINTING:** Squeeze the paint on to a plate, and spread out into a thin and even layer. Dip the 'stamp' in the paint, and test on a piece of paper first; this will help you to work out how much paint and pressure to apply for the fresco itself.

Once you are ready to start, use a long spirit level as a guide, to ensure that the motifs are all positioned in a straight line.

Tip: Step back regularly from the fresco to check that you are happy with the pattern in its entirety.

DYE A SHEEPSKIN PALE PINK

<u>MATERIALS:</u>
large bowl or tub + 1 kg cooking salt + pale pink fabric dye for machine use + latex gloves + natural sheepskin

1. **<u>PREPARE THE DYE:</u>** Fill one third of the bowl with boiling water and mix in the cooking salt and the dye. It is best to do this outside if you can, or in the bath, since the dye can stain easily.

2. **<u>START TO DYE:</u>** Put on the latex gloves and dip the sheepskin into the bowl, turning it over with your hands so that the dye is fully absorbed. Add more water if necessary to ensure that the skin is fully immersed. Soak for approximately an hour, turning over at regular intervals for an even distribution of colour. Take the skin out of the bowl, dispose of the dye and clean the bowl thoroughly. Again, it is best to do this outside if you can. Wring out as much of the excess liquid as possible. The drying phase is time-consuming, not so much because of the wool, but rather due to how long the skin takes to dry. It can be rather slimy and not very nice to handle, but don't panic! It will dry eventually. Leave it flat in direct sunlight for as long as possible, turning over from time to time. You can finish off the drying process in a tumble-drier on a low setting, though take care not to leave it for too long (no more than one hour) since the wool may become matted. Check from time to time.

Tip: It is advisable to dye the sheepskin in the summer, since the drying process will be far less time-consuming!

CREATE COLOUR SAMPLES ON CANVAS

MATERIALS:
4 pre-stretched canvases (approx. 40 × 20 cm) + household paint (in a choice of colours) + small roller + letter and number stamps + black ink

RANGE OF COLOURS ILLUSTRATED:
beige (Dove Tale), yellow (India Yellow), pale pink (Nancy's Blushes), grey (Down Pipe)

1. **PAINT THE CANVASES:** Squeeze the first colour onto a dish and, using the roller, apply a coat of paint to the first canvas. Take care to leave a narrow, white border around the edges. Leave to dry. Repeat the process for the other three canvases, cleaning the roller thoroughly and allowing it dry between each painting.

2. **NUMBER THE CANVASES:** Select a number on your stamp - for example, 'N. 371', 'N. 431', 'N. 850' and so on - then press it into the black ink. Position in the corner of the canvas, and press down firmly. Repeat the process with the remaining canvases. You can easily find stamps such as this in art shops, or buy them from online retailers. Tip: test the stamp out first on a piece of paper before moving on to the canvases.

Shown together the canvases will make a striking addition to your home and will complement the other pictures that you have on display.

CREATE AN ART DECO AMBIANCE WITH PAINTED BIRCH

MATERIALS:
4–5 birch trunks (or similar wood) (approx. 180–200 cm high and 10 cm in diameter)
+ large bowl + white paint + masking tape + paintbrush with large bristles

1. **SOURCING YOUR WOOD:** Approach companies that deal in firewood. They are sure to stock slender trunks of birch, and you will be able to choose from among those that have not already been cut.

2. **PREPARE THE WOOD:** Brush the wood to remove any soil and moss. Clean with some soap and a damp cloth if necessary.

3. **START TO PAINT:** Prepare the paint in a bowl, mixing thoroughly a large spoonful of white paint with two litres of water. Cover each trunk with this mixture for a whitewash finish, dispose of the excess liquid and leave the wood to dry.

Stick masking tape around each trunk at varying levels, from between 35 and 70 cm up from the ends. You could also mark out a small area with two sections of tape to make a stripe. Apply a thick coat of the white paint to each trunk, remove the masking tape and leave to dry.

Lean the trunks against a wall as a decorative feature, taking care to ensure that they are secure and won't topple over.

FRAME VINTAGE WALLPAPER

MATERIALS:
roll of vintage wallpaper + 1 light oak frame (approx. 70 × 50 cm)

1. **CHOOSE YOUR WALLPAPER:** Vintage wallpaper is readily available online and in vintage shops, and can be bought at a cost of between £10 and £30 a roll.

2. **FRAME THE WALLPAPER:** Cut the paper to the same size as the frame and insert behind the glass and close up the back.

Tip: Why not try the same technique using different-sized frames and a variety of vintage wallpaper to make a striking collection that can be displayed as a group?

SOFT
FURNISHINGS

MAKE AND EMBROIDER PEBBLE CUSHIONS

MATERIALS:
grey and khaki wool fabric (50 × 100 cm in each colour) + sewing pins + dressmaker's carbon paper (50 × 50 cm) + pencil + fawn and dark grey embroidery thread + sewing needle + 1 kg cushion stuffing

1. **PREPARE THE FABRIC:** First, cut the fabric. Double over the grey wool and draw an irregular, pebble-shaped circle on top of one half. Pin together and cut out the shape, following the line you have just drawn. Remove the pins. You should have two equal-sized pebbles. Repeat this step for the khaki fabric.

2. **START EMBROIDERING:** Transfer the pebble motif (fig. 13, page 182) onto the grey fabric using a pencil and the carbon paper. Repeat with the khaki fabric, this time drawing a circle motif directly onto the material. It should be off-centre, as illustrated. Take the fawn-coloured thread and separate into strands, retaining two for the sewing. Insert the thread into the needle and chain-stitch (fig. 21, page 190) the pattern onto the grey wool. Repeat for the khaki fabric.

3. **SEW THE CUSHIONS:** the model shown here does not have a removable cover.

   Pin together the two pieces of grey fabric, reverse sides facing out. There is no need to make a hem, since you will be using blanket stitch (fig. 22, page 190) to sew the fabric together. Take the dark grey thread, again separating the strands and retaining two for the sewing. Sew all the way around the cushion, leaving a small gap just large enough to insert the stuffing. Fold the fabric inside out, and fill with as much stuffing as possible, for a firm cushion. Close up the gap with blanket stitch. Repeat this step with the khaki fabric.

TIE-DYE AND EMBROIDER TEA TOWELS

MATERIALS:
2 cotton tea towels + black hand dye + 1 kg cooking salt + large bowl + latex gloves + pencil + dressmaker's carbon paper + embroidery cotton + sewing needle

1. **DYE THE TOWELS:** Dampen the towels and wring out any excess water. Mark a line approximately 15 cm up from the bottom of each towel: this is the section that you will dip into the dye. In the bowl mix together the dye and cooking salt with boiling water. Dip the towels in the dye, taking care not to lower them further than the 15-cm mark. Leave them to soak for about 45 minutes. Wearing the gloves wring out the dye from the towels. Rinse them thoroughly several times. Leave to dry, then iron.

2. **EMBROIDER THE TOWELS:** With a pencil and the carbon paper transfer the diamond pattern (fig. 9, page 181) into the corner of the area that has been dyed. Separate the cotton into strands, and retain two for the sewing. Chain-stitch (fig. 21, page 190) the pattern onto the fabric.

YEARS OF BAUHAUS DESIGN
75 1919 1994

ALVAR AALTO

MAKE GEOMETRIC-PATTERN CUSHIONS

MATERIALS:
fabric with a Scandinavian-style geometric pattern (50 × 150 cm for each cushion) + sewing pins
+ sewing needle + assorted cotton threads + 1–2 kg cushion stuffing + 4 wooden buttons

1. **CUT THE FABRIC:** You will need two rectangles, 62 × 38 cm for each cushion. Allow for an additional 1 cm for the seams.

2. **SEW THE CUSHION:** The cushions illustrated do not have removable covers.

    Pin together the two rectangles, reverse sides out and join with whip stitch: insert the thread through the needle, tie a knot at the end and push through the fabric, 1 cm in from the edges. Take the thread over and under and repeat all the way around, leaving an opening of about 15 cm at the centre of one length for the stuffing. Turn the fabric inside out, and fill with as much stuffing as possible, for a firm cushion. To close the opening, turn in the 1-cm seam and pin both pieces together. Sew with running stitch (fig. 20, page 190).

    Double-thread your needle, and sew a button in the centre of each side of the cushion, passing the thread through several times to make sure that they are firmly attached.

    Repeat for the second cushion.

KNIT
COSY COASTERS

MATERIALS:
fine linen thread + ball of thick hemp string + ball of bulky pale pink wool + 6.5-mm knitting needles

1. **MAKE WOOLLEN COASTERS:** Take together the pink wool and the fine linen thread and cast on 16 stitches. Purl the first row, and knit the second. Repeat until you have 16 rows. Cast off.

2. **MAKE HEMP COASTERS:** Follow the same method using thick hemp, this time without the fine linen thread. The thickness of each should be more or less consistent, as should the size (16 × 16 cm).

EMBROIDER TABLE LINEN

MATERIALS:
tablecloth and table napkins in linen or grey cotton + dressmaker's carbon paper + pencil + sky-blue embroidery cotton + sewing needle

1. **EMBROIDER THE TABLECLOTH:** Photocopy the spiral pattern (fig. 14, page 183), enlarging to the size you require, then transfer to the tablecloth with a pencil and the carbon paper. Separate the thread into strands, and retain two for sewing. Use running stitch (fig. 20, page 190) to sew the pattern.

2. **EMBROIDER THE TABLE NAPKIN:** Trace the half-spiral pattern (fig. 15, page 184) on to the napkin following the same method as for the tablecloth, ensuring that it is lined up to the edge of the fabric. Sew the pattern as before.

Ⓐ × 2

54 cm

54 cm

• fig. 1 •

Ⓑ × 1

26 cm

32 cm

• fig. 2 •

• fig. 3 •

Second fold of 2 cm

First fold
of 1 cm

Seam 1.8 cm
from the top

• fig. 4 •

• fig. 5 •

MAKE A LEAF-PATTERN BAG

MATERIALS:
thick khaki fabric (100 × 150 cm) + grosgrain ribbon (100 cm in length, and no less than 3 cm in width) + cotton thread + potato + Stanley knife + textile paint (almond green and blue) + iron

1. **CUT THE CLOTH:** Cut two 'A'-sized rectangles (fig. 1) and one 'B'-sized rectangle (fig. 2). These dimensions allow for a seam of 1 cm and a hem of 3 cm. Whip stitch (see page 151) the fabric edges to prevent fraying.

    Cut the grosgrain in half to make two handles each 50 cm long, and whipstitch the ends.

2. **SEW THE BAG BODY:** Using running stitch (fig. 20, page 190) sew together the lengths of rectangles A, reverse sides out. Make sure to leave a seam of 1 cm.

    Tip: A hand-stitched bag will make a great decorative piece, but you will need to use a sewing machine if you want your bag to transport any weight.

3. **MAKE THE BASE OF THE BAG:** fold rectangle B along the width, right sides out. Cut 8-mm notches in the corners of the bag body (fig. 3) so that the seams can be more easily pinned to the base of the bag. Sew body and base together, leaving a 1-cm seam. Turn the piece right side out.

4. **MAKE THE TOP HEM:** make two successive folds along the top of the bag, first 1 cm from the fabric edge, then 2 cm. Iron and sew a hem 1.8 cm from the top of the bag (fig. 4).

5. **ATTACH THE HANDLES:** Pin the handles to the bag, ensuring that the ends are 16 cm apart, 2 cm down from the top edge, and at an equal distance from the sides. Sew to fix in place (fig. 5).

6. **MAKE THE PATTERN:** Cut a potato in two. Dispose of one half and draw the leaf motif (fig. 11, page 181) on top of the other. Use a Stanley knife to cut away the excess, and soak up any starch with a kitchen towel. Next, pour the blue textile paint onto a plate and spread out into a thin, even layer. Dip the stamp in the paint. Do a test print on a piece of paper before moving on to the bag. When you are ready, place the bag on a firm, level surface and, using a pencil, mark a vertical line down the centre. Now start printing, using the leaf pattern (fig. 12, page 181) as a guide. Once you have completed your pattern in blue, repeat the process with the green paint (as illustrated). Leave to dry. To fix the paint, run a hot non-steam iron over the surface of the bag.

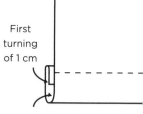

First
turning
of 1 cm

Second turning of 2 cm

• fig. 1 •

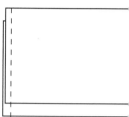

• fig. 2 •

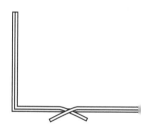

• fig. 3 •

CREATE A FLORAL-PATTERN CUSHION

MATERIALS:
fabric with a Scandinavian-style floral print (50 × 150 cm) + sewing needle + assorted cotton threads + yellow piping (2 m in length) + cushion pad (40 × 40 cm)

1. **CUT THE FABRIC:** Cut a square measuring 42 × 42 cm and two rectangles measuring 42 × 35 cm. Whip stitch (see page 151) the edges.

2. **SEW THE CUSHIONS:** Take one of the rectangles and, on one length, turn under by 1 cm, then 2 cm, to form a hem (fig. 1). Sew in running stitch to secure (fig. 20, page 190). Place one rectangle on top of the other, right sides up with the hemmed edge on top, so that the total width is 42 cm. Pin and sew together (fig. 2).

Take the square measuring 42 × 42 cm right side up and, using a sewing machine, attach the yellow piping to the edges. Finish by crossing over the ends of the piping (fig. 3).

Take the rectangle and place it on top of the square, both with right sides in, so that the piping sits in-between the two. Pin and sew together, restitching around the seam that you made before. Turn the work right side out and use a needle to push out the corners. Insert the cushion pad.

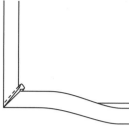

• fig. 1 •

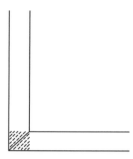

• fig. 2 •

SEW A SNUG BLANKET

MATERIALS:
Cream-coloured fake fur (150 × 250 cm) + cream-coloured cotton fabric (150 × 400 cm) + sewing needle + assorted threads + almond green embroidery cotton + potato + Stanley knife + almond green textile paint + iron

1. **CUT THE FABRIC:** Wash the cotton fabric before you start in case it shrinks a little. Cut a rectangle 250 × 150 cm from the fake fur, and from the cotton fabric (this includes the 1-cm seam required). Whip stitch (see page 151) the edges of the cotton.

   Next, cut 15-cm strips from the remaining cotton to make a total length of 8 m.

2. **SEW THE COVER:** Sew together the cotton and fake fur rectangles, right sides out, 1 cm from the edge of the fabric.

   Sew the 15-cm bands of cotton together end to end. Iron to open the seams then fold and iron the entire strip lengthwise.

   Sandwich the large rectangle into the folded band of fabric. The edges remain raw. Pin and sew 1 cm from the edges to join. At the corners, fold under the excess and use running-stitch (fig. 20, page 190) along each side of the diagonal join (fig. 1).

   Separate the almond green cotton into strands, retaining one strand for sewing. Make several lines in running stitch to form a square in the corner (fig. 2).

3. **MAKE A CROSS STAMP FOR THE COTTON BAND:** Cut a potato in half. Carve out the cross (fig. 3, page 177) with the Stanley knife and dispose of the excess. Use a kitchen towel to absorb any starch.

   Squeeze the textile paint on to a dish and spread out into a thin, even layer. Try the stamp out first on a piece of paper. When you are ready, apply the stamp to the cotton band at 7-cm intervals. Work on a firm, flat surface to ensure that pressure is evenly applied. Fix the paint by running a hot, steamless iron over the surface.

BRIGHTEN UP BED LINEN

MATERIALS:
duvet cover and pillowcase in white cotton + 1 potato + Stanley knife + textile paint (a choice of 3 colours) + pencil + ruler + iron

1. **PREPARE THE STAMP:** Cut the potato in two, dispose of one half and carve the triangle motif (fig. 10, page 181) into the other with a Stanley knife. Use a kitchen towel to absorb any excess starch. Squeeze the textile paint onto a plate and spread out into a thin, even layer. Dip the stamp in to the paint, and test out on a piece of paper first, before moving on to the duvet cover and pillowcase.

2. **START PAINTING:** Place the duvet cover on a flat, stable surface. With a pencil mark out the area that you will be stamping: it should be no more than 25 cm from the top of the and 35 cm from the sides. Stamp the first row of triangles, taking care to position them in a straight line. When you are ready to try a different colour, wash and dry the stamp, and repeat the process. You can use a ruler as a guide while printing, to ensure that there are no gaps or irregularities in any of the rows.

Next, work on the pillowcase. Mark the area you wish to print, ensuring that is no less than 5 cm from the top or bottom (the pattern can continue right to the edges, as illustrated). Now print 5 rows of triangles using the same method as for the duvet cover. Allow the paint to dry, then iron to fix.

• fig. 1 •

• fig. 2 •

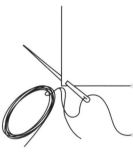

• fig. 3 •

• fig. 4 •

MAKE GOATSKIN AND PRINTED CUSHIONS

MATERIALS:

For the goatskin cushion: small goatskin + Scandinavian-style black-and-white fabric (50 cm in length) + needle + assorted cotton threads + cushion stuffing

For the printed cushion: Scandinavian-style black-and-white fabric (50 cm in length) + needle + assorted cotton threads + cushion stuffing + ball of fine black wool

1. **CUT THE FABRIC:** For the larger cushion cut a rectangle from the printed fabric, 47 × 37 cm (this includes the 1-cm required for the seams). Whip stitch (see page 151) the edges of the rectangle.

   Cut a rectangle of goatskin to the same size, 47 × 37 cm.

2. **SEW THE GOATSKIN CUSHION:** Position one rectangle on top of the other, insides out, and sew together, using either a long stitch on a sewing machine or running stitch (fig. 20, page 190), leaving a space of about 15 cm at the centre of one length. Turn inside out and insert as much stuffing as possible for a firm cushion. To close the remaining gap, turn-in the 1-cm seam on both sides, pin together and sew with running stitch.

3. **SEW THE SMALL PRINTED CUSHION:** Cut two rectangles from the printed fabric, 35 × 25 cm (this includes the 1-cm seams). Whip stitch the edges.

   Position one rectangle on top of the other, insides facing in, and sew together, leaving a space of about 10 cm at the centre of one length. Turn inside out and insert as much stuffing as possible. To close the remaining gap, turn-in the 1-cm seam, pin together and sew with running stitch.

4. **MAKE THE POMPOMS:** Wind twenty loops of wool round three of your fingers, so the loop is about 5 cm in diameter (fig. 1). Cut a piece of wool 25 cm long and pass it through the loop, then tie three tight knots (fig. 2).

   Use a needle and thread to fix the wool to the corner of the cushion, then tie three more knots while adding the two threads to the remainder of the pompom (fig. 3). Take another piece of wool 30 cm long, and make five tight loops round the pompom, followed by three more tight knots (fig. 4).

   Open out the pompom by cutting off the bottom. Make three more like this for the other corners of the cushion.

TABLEWARE

CREATE SPIRAL-PATTERN PLATES

MATERIALS:
white china dessert plates + pencil + carbon paper + black porcelain paint pen

1. **PREPARE THE PLATES:** Wash the plates with soap and hot water to remove any grease. Rinse, then dry thoroughly.

2. **PAINT THE PATTERN:** Transfer the pattern (fig. 16, page 185) on to the first plate using a pencil and carbon paper. Remove the paper and draw over the lines with the black pen. Repeat this process with the remaining plates. To fix the paint, place the plates in a reheated oven at 100°C (gas mark 3-4) for 30 minutes. Avoid cleaning them in a dishwasher as this may damage the paint.

Tip: Avoid using plates that are very hollow, since it will be more difficult to trace the pattern using the carbon paper. Opt for flat ones if you can and fix the paper in place with masking tape if necessary.

EMBELLISH CERAMIC POTS WITH A FLORAL MOTIF

MATERIALS:
grey china pots + pencil + carbon paper + black and light grey porcelain paint pens

1. **PREPARE THE POTS:** Wash the pots with soap and hot water to remove any grease. Rinse, then dry thoroughly.

2. **PAINT THE PATTERN:** Transfer the pattern (fig. 17, page 186) on to the first pot using a pencil and carbon paper. You can use masking tape to secure the carbon paper to the pot if necessary. Remove the paper and draw over the lines with the black pen.

Repeat, this time using the grey pen, and continue in this manner until you have equal numbers in each colour. To fix the paint place the pots in a preheated oven at 100°C (gas mark 3-4) for 30 minutes. Avoid cleaning the pots in a dishwasher, as this may damage the paint.

ADD A DECORATIVE DESIGN TO SMALL CHINA BOWLS

MATERIALS:
small white china bowls + pencil + carbon paper + blue porcelain paint pen

1. **PREPARE THE BOWLS:** Wash the bowls with soap and hot water to remove any grease. Rinse, then dry thoroughly.

2. **PAINT THE PATTERN:** Transfer the pattern (fig. 18, page 187) on to the first bowl using a pencil and carbon paper. Use masking tape to secure the carbon paper to the bowl if necessary. Remove the paper and draw over the lines with the blue pen. Repeat the process with the remaining bowls. To fix the paint, place the bowls in a preheated oven at 100°C (gas mark 3-4) for 30 minutes. Avoid cleaning the bowls in a dishwasher as this may damage the paint.

PAINT POLKA-DOT TUMBLERS

MATERIALS:
glass tumblers + pencil + carbon paper + transparent beige glass paint + 1 fine paint brush

1. **PREPARE THE TUMBLERS:** Wash the tumblers with soap and hot water to remove any grease. Rinse, then dry thoroughly.

2. **PAINT THE PATTERN:** Transfer the pattern (fig. 19, page 187) on to the first tumbler using a pencil and carbon paper. Use masking tape to secure the carbon paper to the tumbler if necessary. Remove the paper and paint over the dots with the glass paint. Repeat the process with the remaining tumblers. To fix the paint, place the tumblers in the oven at 160°C (gas mark 4) and leave for 45 minutes. Avoid cleaning the tumblers in a dishwasher as this may damage the paint.

TEMPLATES AND MOTIFS

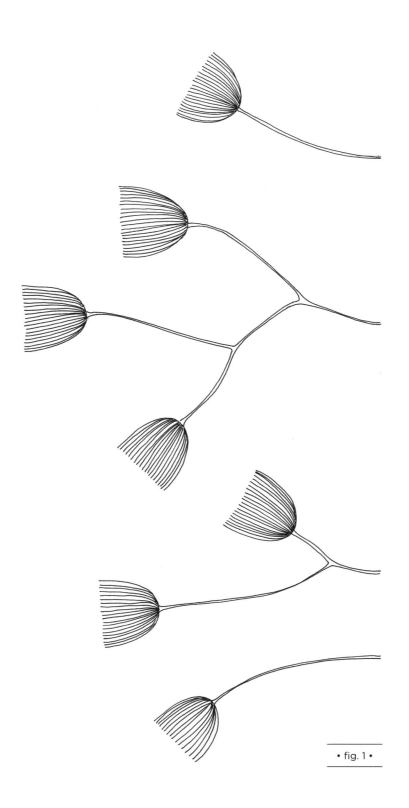

• fig. 1 •

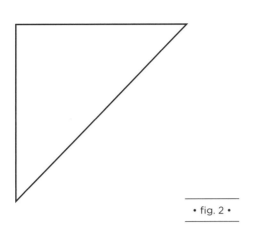

• fig. 2 •

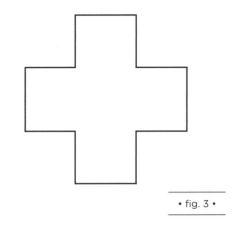

• fig. 3 •

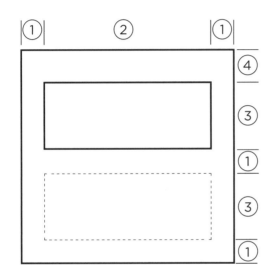

1. Thickness
2. Length
3. Width
4. 5-cm overlap

• fig. 4 •

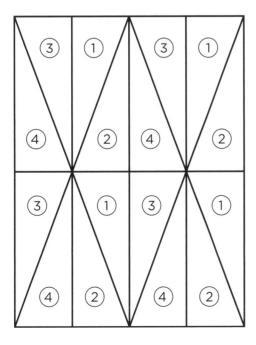

1. Greyish-beige
2. Ecru
3. Pink
4. Green

• fig. 5 •

• fig. 6 •

• fig. 7 •

• fig. 8 •

• fig. 9 •

• fig. 10 •

• fig. 11 •

• fig. 12 •

181

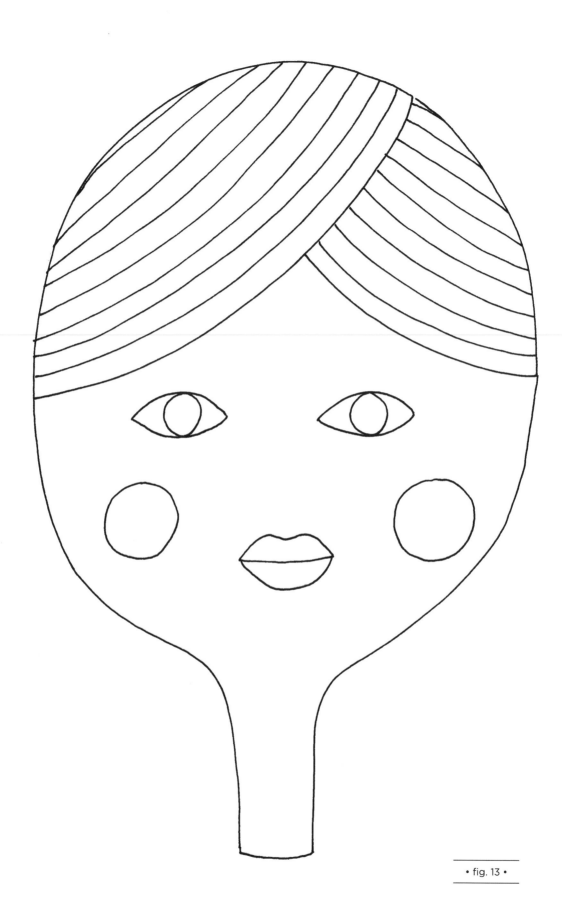

• fig. 13 •

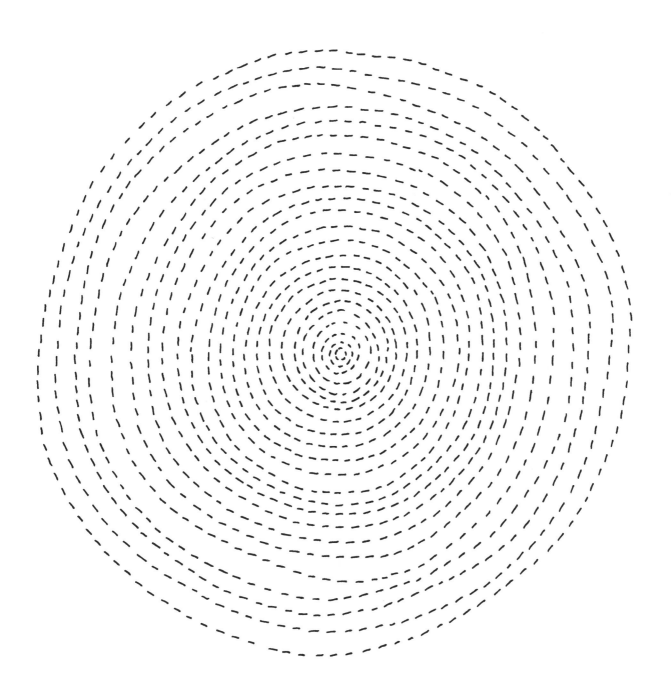

• fig. 14 •

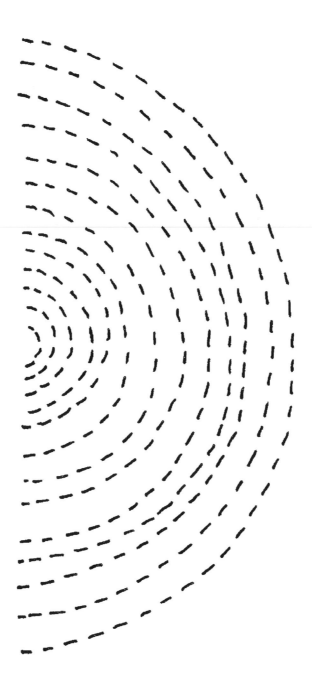

• fig. 15 •

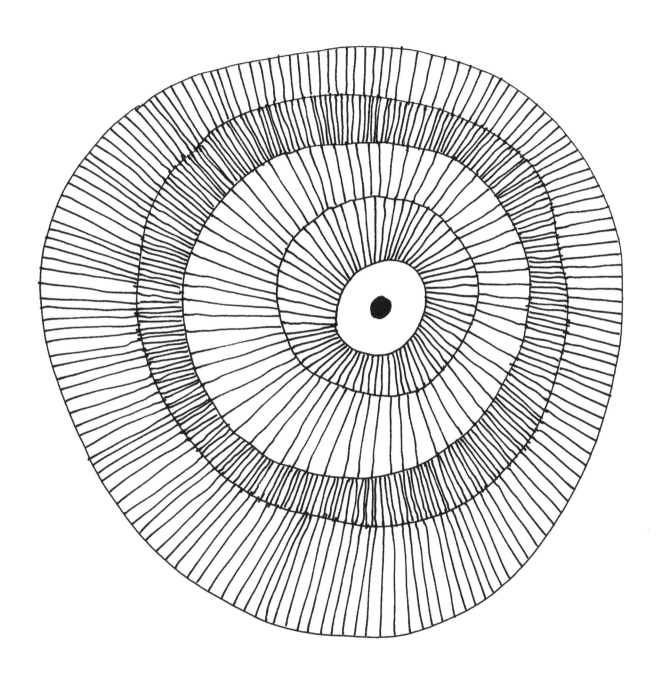

• fig. 16 •

• fig. 17 •

• fig. 18 •

• fig. 19 •

COLOUR CHART

ALMOND GREEN: TERESA'S GREEN

BLACK: OFF BLACK

GREY: DOWN PIPE

YELLOW: INDIA YELLOW

BLUE: STIFFKEY BLUE

KHAKI GREEN: OLIVE

ECRU: SKIMMING STONE

PINK: CALAMINE

PATTERN CHART

BELOW ARE A SMALL SELECTION OF SCANDINAVIAN PATTERNS THAT
YOU CAN USE IN YOUR DESIGNS

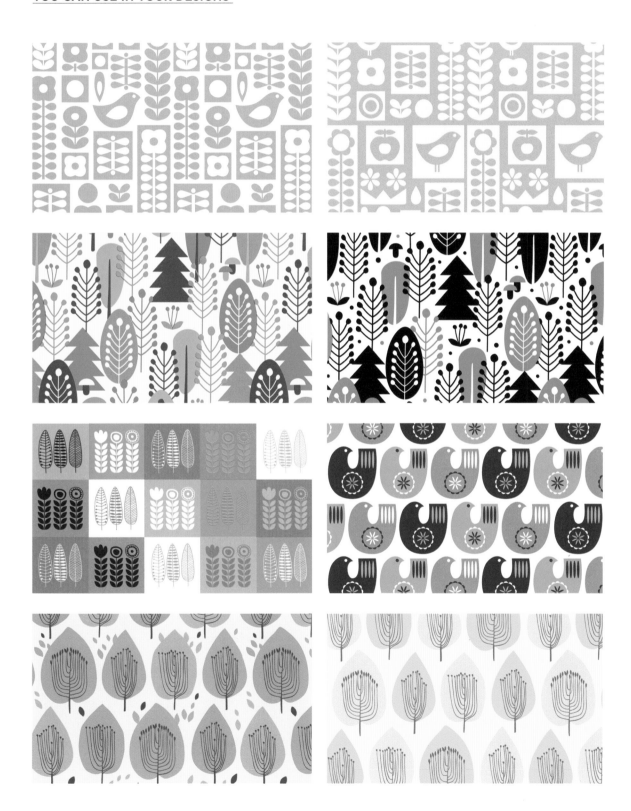

BASIC EMBROIDERY STITCHES

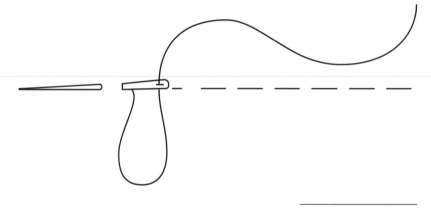

• fig. 20 • running stitch

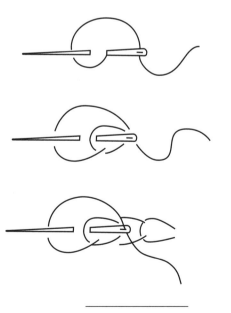

• fig. 21 • chain stitch

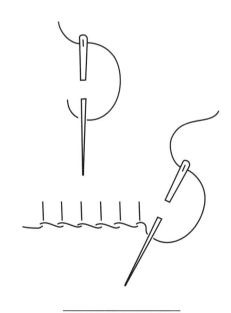

• fig. 22 • blanket stitch

INDEX

Page numbers in italics refer to illustrations

ACKNOWLEDGMENTS

FARROW&BALL paints were used in all the designs illustrated in this book

www.farrow-ball.com

My thanks to Cécile & Olivier, Annabelle & Yves-Marie, who opened wide the doors
of their homes so that we could take our photos.

PICTURE CREDITS

p. 17: © Picture Press/Janne Peters/Studio X; p. 18: © Picture Press/Janne Peters/Studio X; p. 39 (bottom right): © DeAgostini/Leemage; pp. 30–31: © Picture Press/Jonas von der Hude/Studio X; p. 40 (top left): © DeAgostini/Leemage; p. 64 (top): Photograph © P & T Ibsen; pp. 74–75 : © Fotolia/gemenacom; p. 90: © Picture Press/Stefan Thurmann/Studio X; p. 91: © Picture Press/Stefan Thurmann/Studio X; p. 92 (bottom right): © Picture Press/Jonas von der Hude/Studio X; p. 93: © Picture Press/Julia Hoersch/ Studio X; p. 94: © Living4media/Studio X; p. 95: © Picture Press/Jonas von der Hude/Studio X; p. 96: © Picture Press/Sabrina Rothe/Studio X; p. 97 (bottom left): © Picture Press/Julia Hoersch/Studio X; p. 97 (right): © Picture Press/Jonas von der Hude/Studio X; p. 97 (top left): © Living4media/Studio X; p. 99: © Andrew Boyd/Living4media/Studio X; p. 104: © Picture Press/Jonas von der Hude/Studio X; pp. 110–74: Photographies: © Frédéric Lucano/stylisme: Sonia Lucano; p. 189 (top left and bottom right): © Fotolia/Yaviki, © Fotolia/Yaviki, © Fotolia/Silmen, © Fotolia/Silmen, © Fotolia/Rebekka Ivacson, © Fotolia/Rebekka Ivacson, © Fotolia/Silmen, © Fotolia/Silmen.

Translated from the French *Esprit Scandinave* by David Wilson

First published in the United Kingdom in 2016 by
Thames & Hudson Ltd, 181A High Holborn,
London WC1V 7QX

Original edition © 2015 Hachette Livre (Hachette Pratique), Paris
This edition © 2015 Thames & Hudson Ltd, London

British Library Cataloguing-in-Publication Data
A catalogue record for this book is available from the British Library

ISBN 978-0-500-29239-6

Printed and bound in Spain

To find out about all our publications, please visit **www.thamesandhudson.com**. There you can subscribe to our e-newsletter, browse or download our current catalogue, and buy any titles that are in print.